Terror

Mark P. Worell

In this short text, Worrell shines a unique, unorthodox light on "terror" from the standpoint of critical social theory. He explains how the social, political, and economic effects of terrorism fit into the dynamics and structures of the modern world as a whole. This book is for social problems and sociology of terrorism courses.

Mark P. Worrell teaches sociological theory and courses in politics, religion, and culture at the State University of New York at Cortland.

University Readers
Reading Materials Evolved.

THE SOCIAL ISSUES
COLLECTION™

Routledge
Taylor & Francis Group

Framing 21st Century Social Issues

The goal of this new, unique Series is to offer readable, teachable "thinking frames" on today's social problems and social issues by leading scholars. These are available for view on http://routledge.custom-gateway.com/routledge-social-issues.html.

For instructors teaching a wide range of courses in the social sciences, the Routledge *Social Issues Collection* now offers the best of both worlds: originally written short texts that provide "overviews" to important social issues *as well as* teachable excerpts from larger works previously published by Routledge and other presses.

As an instructor, click to the website to view the library and decide how to build your custom anthology and which thinking frames to assign. Students can choose to receive the assigned materials in print and/or electronic formats at an affordable price.

Available

Body Problems
Running and Living Long in a Fast-Food Society
Ben Agger

Sex, Drugs, and Death
Addressing Youth Problems in American
Society
Tammy Anderson

The Stupidity Epidemic
Worrying About Students, Schools, and
America's Future
Joel Best

Empire Versus Democracy
The Triumph of Corporate and Military
Power
Carl Boggs

Contentious Identities
Ethnic, Religious, and Nationalist Conflicts in
Today's World
Daniel Chirot

The Future of Higher Education
Dan Clawson and Max Page

Waste and Consumption
Capitalism, the Environment, and the Life of
Things
Simonetta Falasca-Zamponi

Rapid Climate Change
Causes, Consequences, and Solutions
Scott G. McNall

**The Problem of Emotions
in Societies**
Jonathan H. Turner

Outsourcing the Womb
Race, Class, and Gestational Surrogacy in a
Global Market
France Winddance Twine

**Changing Times for Black
Professionals**
Adia Harvey Wingfield

First published 2013
by Routledge
711 Third Avenue, New York, NY 10017

Simultaneously published in the UK
by Routledge
2 Park Square, Milton Park, Abingdon, Oxon OX14 4RN

Routledge is an imprint of the Taylor & Francis Group, an informa business

© 2013 Taylor & Francis

The right of Mark P. Worrell to be identified as author of this work has been
asserted by him in accordance with sections 77 and 78 of the Copyright, Designs
and Patents Act 1988.

All rights reserved. No part of this book may be reprinted or reproduced or
utilized in any form or by any electronic, mechanical, or other means, now known
or hereafter invented, including photocopying and recording, or in any information
storage or retrieval system, without permission in writing from the publishers.

Trademark Notice: Product or corporate names may be trademarks or
registered trademarks, and are used only for identification and explanation without
intent to infringe.

Library of Congress Cataloging-in-Publication Data
Worrell, Mark P.
Terror: social, political, and economic perspectives / Mark P. Worrell.
   p. cm. — (Framing 21st century social issues)
Includes bibliographical references and index.
ISBN 978-0-415-52032-4 (pbk.: alk. paper) — ISBN 978-0-203-07378-0
(ebook: alk. paper) 1. Terrorism—Social aspects. 2. Terrorism—Political
aspects. 3. Terrorism—Economic aspects. I. Title.
HV6431.W69 2012
363.325—dc23   2012026765

ISBN: 978-0-415-52032-4 (pbk)
ISBN: 978-0-203-07378-0 (ebk)

Typeset in Garamond and Gill sans
by Cenveo Publisher Services

University Readers (www.universityreaders.com): Since 1992, University
Readers has been a leading custom publishing service, providing reasonably priced,
copyright-cleared, course pachs, custom textbooks, and custom publishing services
in print and digital formats to thousands of professors nationwide. The Routledge
Custom Gateway provides easy access to thousands of readings from hundreds of
books and articles via an online library. The partnership of University Readers and
Routledge brings custom publishing expertise and deep academic content together
to help professors create perfect course materials that are affordable for students.

Terror
Social, Political, and Economic Perspectives

Mark P. Worrell
State University of New York, Cortland

Routledge
Taylor & Francis Group

NEW YORK AND LONDON

Why Nations Go to War
A Sociology of Military Conflict
Mark P. Worrell

**How Ethical Systems Change:
Eugenics, the Final
Solution, Bioethics**
Sheldon Ekland-Olson and Julie Beicken

**How Ethical Systems Change:
Abortion and Neonatal Care**
Sheldon Ekland-Olson and Elyshia Aseltine

**How Ethical Systems Change:
Tolerable Suffering and Assisted Dying**
Sheldon Ekland-Olson and Elyshia Aseltine

**How Ethical Systems Change:
Lynching and Capital Punishment**
Sheldon Ekland-Olson and Danielle Dirks

**Nuclear Family Values, Extended
Family Lives: The Power of Race,
Class, and Gender**
Natalia Sarkisian and Naomi Gerstel

**Disposable Youth, Racialized
Memories, and the Culture of Cruelty**
Henry Giroux

**Due Process Denied: Detentions and
Deportations in the United States**
Tanya Golash-Boza

**Oversharing: Presentation of
Self in the Internet Age**
Ben Agger

**Foreign Remedies: What the
Experience of Other Nations
Can Tell Us about Next Steps in
Reforming U.S. Health Care**
David A. Rochefort and Kevin P. Donnelly

**DIY: The Search for Control and
Self-Reliance in the 21st Century**
Kevin Wehr

Forthcoming

**Torture: A Sociology of Violence and
Human Rights**
Lisa Hajjar

Are We Coddling Prisoners?
Benjamin Fleury-Steiner

Identity Problems in the Facebook Era
Daniel Trottier

Trafficking and Terror
Pardis Mahdavi

Beyond the Prison Industrial Complex
Kevin Wehr and Elyshia Aseltine

Color Line?
Krystal Beamon

Is Working Longer the Answer?
Tay McNamara and John Williamson

iTime
Ben Agger

Contents

〰〜〰

Contents

Series Foreword

The world in the early 21st century is beset with problems—a troubled economy, global warming, oil spills, religious and national conflict, poverty, HIV, health problems associated with sedentary lifestyles. Virtually no nation is exempt, and everyone, even in affluent countries, feels the impact of these global issues.

Since its inception in the 19th century, sociology has been the academic discipline dedicated to analyzing social problems. It is still so today. Sociologists offer not only diagnoses; they glimpse solutions, which they then offer to policy makers and citizens who work for a better world. Sociology played a major role in the civil rights movement during the 1960s in helping us to understand racial inequalities and prejudice, and it can play a major role today as we grapple with old and new issues.

This series builds on the giants of sociology, such as Weber, Durkheim, Marx, Parsons, and Mills. It uses their frames, and newer ones, to focus on particular issues of contemporary concern. These books are about the nuts and bolts of social problems, but they are equally about the frames through which we analyze these problems. It is clear by now that there is no single correct way to view the world, but only paradigms, models, which function as lenses through which we peer. For example, in analyzing oil spills and environmental pollution, we can use a frame that views such outcomes as unfortunate results of a reasonable effort to harvest fossil fuels. "Drill, baby, drill" sometimes involves certain costs as pipelines rupture and oil spews forth. Or we could analyze these environmental crises as inevitable outcomes of our effort to dominate nature in the interest of profit. The first frame would solve oil spills with better environmental protection measures and clean-ups, while the second frame would attempt to prevent them altogether, perhaps shifting away from the use of petroleum and natural gas and toward alternative energies that are "green."

These books introduce various frames such as these for viewing social problems. They also highlight debates between social scientists who frame problems differently. The books suggest solutions, both on the macro and micro levels. That is, they suggest what new policies might entail, and they also identify ways in which people, from the ground level, can work toward a better world, changing themselves and their lives and families and providing models of change for others.

Readers do not need an extensive background in academic sociology to benefit from these books. Each book is student-friendly in that we provide glossaries of terms for the uninitiated that are keyed to bolded terms in the text. Each chapter ends with questions for further thought and discussion. The level of each book is accessible to undergraduate students, even as these books offer sophisticated and innovative analyses.

This is the third year of our Routledge Social Issues book series. These brief books explore key contemporary social problems in ways that introduce basic concepts in the social sciences, cover key literature in the field, and offer original analyses and diagnoses. Our series includes books on topics ranging widely from global warming, to global ethnic conflict, to comparative health care, to oversharing on the Internet. These readable treatments can be assigned in both lower- and upper-division sociology courses in which instructors seek affordable, pithy treatments of social problems.

Our series is framed by our increasingly global world in which economic inequalities produce political and military conflicts. In this imaginative book, Mark P. Worrell examines one of the manifestations of this conflict: terrorism. Since 9/11 it has been difficult to celebrate globalization without acknowledging that terror has become global, an issue that Worrell takes up. No one is immune, or invulnerable, even as talking about "terrorism" somehow normalizes it.

Preface

Presently, "terrorism" consists almost entirely of Sunni extremists killing other Muslims in Islamic countries (The National Counterterrorism Center 2012: 13–14); therefore, investigations that deviate from this fact would seem to be missing the point. The unofficial motto of positivistic sociology is "what you see is what you get," but critical social theory runs in an entirely opposite direction: what we see on the surface (members of group X killing members of group Y for reasons A, B, and C) overlooks the primary drivers operating in the background that set groups into violent reaction. The primary global driver right now and in the foreseeable future is American military power deployed around the planet in order to shore up U.S. political dominance and, ultimately, enhance and preserve dollar supremacy.

My aim is to shine a unique, synthetic, and heterodox light on "terror" in the age of American imperial hegemony from the standpoint of critical social theory, broadly conceived. Few specialists seem to have noticed that the birth of the modern age of terrorism coincides with the breakdown in one regime of capital accumulation and the rise of another that depends upon, like never before, the preeminence of speculative financial functions wedded to brute military power. Naturally, given the extreme limitations in size, this essay cannot hope to provide sweeping historical-comparative panoramas, comprehensive literature reviews, or empirical excursions into the contingencies of particular terrorist cells; least of all is this a generic review of terrorism studies. Why, then, examine terror from the standpoint of U.S. political and economic policy at the expense of other relevant positions?

The bourgeoisie of the 17th and 18th centuries were champions of constitutional democracy, liberalism, and other progressive ideals that we still hold dear. However, by the 19th century, industrial capitalism had not only undermined the authority of traditional and reactionary institutions but also liquidated the notions of personal restraint and reasoned social regulation. By the time that the bourgeoisie had gained the upper hand, the idea of freedom from tyranny had already devolved into a concept of *absolute freedom* of the individual and unrestrained accumulation of wealth. The results included periodic and unprecedented economic and social disasters, large-scale wars, etc., alternating with periods of incomprehensible wealth creation for a few. The Great

- Unprecedented political scandals (Watergate and the impeachment of Nixon) and the diminishment of public confidence in the federal government;
- The scuttling of the international gold standard and its replacement by a "Treasury bill standard" (Hudson 2003: 377);
- Recurring waves of governmental deregulation;
- Jettisoning of progressive taxation and the propagation of an **ideology** of egoism and the fantasy of mass-manufacturing millionaires;
- Dismantling of the public welfare system;
- The birth of derivatives trading and the primacy of reckless financial gambling over rational investments (Krier 2008; McNally 2011);
- Growing confidence and proliferation of right-wing fundamentalist Christianity in the United States (Hedges 2006);
- A shift from finite, periodic, and concrete conflicts that can be "won" or "lost" (World War II, Korea, Vietnam) to permanent, open-ended wars against abstractions (terror) where winning and losing are no longer measurable and the "enemy" is equally everywhere and nowhere.

In short, as post-war America began to crumble, capital's rebellion against limits and responsibility took off. Capital looked for its salvation in financial services, domestic repression, hyper-militarism, and the construction of a political–theological "evil other" to combat into eternity. America remade itself into a restive **empire** driven by the spirit of limitlessness.

As this world force tears up and reorganizes the rest of the planet to suit its own interests it unleashes asymmetrical currents of violent, countervailing reaction that likewise reflect the spirit of limitlessness and the desire for counteracting over-regulation. In the United States it is possible to observe this spirit of immoderation communicated from many angles. The self-destructive reaction on the part of millions to the possibility of global climate change, for example, signifies disdain for limits that may intrude upon customary forms of life. Rational analysis is countered by apathy, disavowals, conspiracy theories, and even death threats aimed at climate scientists. From a purely negative point of view, the perplexing and self-defeating acquiescence to seemingly never-ending wars also reflects an accommodation to limitlessness on the part of the American public. Externally, when we observe with dismay the carnage precipitated by, e.g., an Islamic suicide bomber, we are witnessing the same spirit of limitlessness played out in one dramatic moment of personal desperation and devotion. What is important to keep in mind is that if a destructive empire was able to look in a mirror it would not see a direct, undistorted reflection of itself but would have projected back precisely the kind of image offered up by the suicide bomber. In the complex language of critical theory we see here the *speculative relation* between a big object and its little symptomatic other. Britain and the US are the only political entities that have worked themselves up to the status of what we might call modern hegemonic empires in that they exert political, economic, and ideological domination of national and regional blocs (Go 2011), but unbridled passions and impatience with limitations (aspects of what sociologists refer to as **anomie**) have plagued empires and its subjects throughout history.

When the sociologist Emile Durkheim examined the bellicose mentality of imperial Germany he discovered that its essential trait was a delirious, energetic "spiritual state" that he called "a morbid hypertrophy of the will, a kind of will mania" (1915: 44). Reflecting on the acts of terrorists we have no difficulty perceiving a genuinely maniacal disregard for the principles of reality or international law. It is as if our terrorist enemies aspire not merely negatively to the destruction of America or the West (obviously impossible) but positively to the realization of an imaginary empire of utopian purity (also equally impossible). However, this relation between us and them, good and evil, democracy versus totalitarianism, is truly problematic and goes well beyond victims and perpetrators. It may very well be the case that what we perceive in our enemies is, to a certain extent, a distorted reflection of our own imaginations and problems. Perhaps the "will mania" of the terrorist is a symptom of our own collective anomie. A clear-eyed view of American foreign policy with an eye toward the current war on terror appears to coincide very well with Durkheim's description of the "morbid hypertrophy of the will."

> The normal, healthy will, however vigorous, accepts the necessary relations of dependence inherent in the nature of things. Man is part of a physical system which supports, but at the same time limits him, and keeps him in a state of dependence. He therefore submits to the laws of this system, for he cannot change them; he obeys them, even when he makes them serve his ends. For to free himself entirely from these limitations and resistances, he would have to make a vacuum around him, to place himself, that is to say, outside the conditions of life. But there are moral forces equally incumbent on nations and on individuals, though on different grounds and in different ways. There is no State so powerful that it can govern eternally against the wishes of its subjects and force them, by purely external coercion, to submit to its will. There is no state so great that it is not merged in the vaster system formed by the agglomeration of other states, that does not, in other words, form part of the great human community, and owe respect to this. There is a universal conscience and a universal opinion, and it is no more possible to escape the empire of these than to escape the empire of physical laws; for they are forces which re-act against those who transgress them; a State cannot subsist when all humanity is arrayed against it.
>
> (ibid.: 44–45)

America's own brand of "will mania" is reflected, I will argue, in our conceptions of terror and, at least in great part, drives our ongoing military adventures (what was until recently billed as the "war on terror") in both their external and internal phases. Moreover, and this is very important, the contradictions and polar oppositions found rarely at the level of personal and small group psychology find ways of combining at the aggregate levels of political economy and foreign policy. "Will mania" or anomie in one of its aspects combines at the "transcendental" level of the war on terror with an *authoritarian* "will to power" and a drive toward massive violence and *destruction*. Normally, as we will see later, authoritarianism (the paradoxical and simultaneous desire for submission and domination) does not alloy with destructiveness within the individual psyche; authoritarianism and destructiveness are two separate "strategies" for dealing with the turbulence and anxieties of the modern world. Either the threatened person seeks to bond with something stronger while controlling something weaker or the person attempts to annihilate offending objects. When we synthesize these three separate currents of anomie, authoritarianism, and destructiveness at a higher scale of social reality, however, we find a unique double-sided "product" that is greater than and different from the sum of its parts. It will be the task of this book to bring the sociological eye to bear on the problem of terror and terrorism as a particular manifestation of this synthesis. This examination will require not only an account of the terrorist but the empire that opposes it and an excursion through the domains of politics, economy, and religion.

event even though tens of thousands died under the guillotine. Even though an academic consensus has been attempted a time or two there is still disagreement among scholars as to what the problem actually consists of. For concise surveys, see Gibbs (1989), Crenshaw (2011: 21–33), and especially Goodwin's extensive overview (2006). Definitional impasse is likely permanent (Laqueur 1999) because there is no such thing as terrorism once and for all. The notion of terrorism per se obscures its perspectival, contextual, and historical nature. Terror "has been used for the preservation of the status quo and for its overthrow, for the streamlining of a declining society and for the release of new political and economic forces" (Marcuse 1972: 196). Context dependency also lies behind the familiar phrase "One man's terrorist is another man's freedom fighter." For more on this exact phrase and its limitations see Wieviorka (1995: 598). We can examine any number of groups that, prima facie, seem to be more or less identical at least in their methods but "[i]n the spectrum of terrorism, there is a wide variety of causes, actors, and motivations. Each group must be analyzed in its own unique historical, political, and cultural context, for beneath the general features in common, terrorist groups and organizations differ remarkably" (Post, Ruby and Shaw 2002: 110).

Though the term resists final determination, it *can* be pinned down to some degree so long as we are conscious of its fluid and multi-dimensional nature. Departing from standard academic procedure, however, I will resist the urge to condense terror or terrorism into bite-sized definitions here at the beginning. Hopefully, at the end, we will be in a better position to encapsulate the essence of the problem.

Academic interest in terrorism took off in the seventies and throughout the eighties and early nineties scholars constructed a set of definitions and case studies that focused a good deal on paramilitary groups (Rubenstein 1987: 6). The classic picture of terrorism in the 20th century that emerged during this time is one in which groups use violence or the threat of violence against a variety of targets, usually non-combatants or innocent bystanders as well as infrastructure and property, in order to instill fear and communicate a message through the media to an otherwise unresponsive audience for the purpose of eliciting some change in the distribution of power and rewards within a social system. Unlike simple criminals that may use terrorist methods or techniques for purely self-serving ends, terrorist groups are thought of as not being "in it" for the money or for personal gain but are supposedly devoted to ideals such as national liberation, the desire for ethnic or religious recognition and self-determination, or the restoration of some long-lost, imaginary moral order. Recourse to terroristic methods is arrived at when normal channels of discourse, persuasion, and activism are experienced as unproductive, counterproductive, or futile. However, what happens to be labeled as "terroristic" depends greatly on ideas regarding authority.

As sociologists, we should employ a "hermeneutic of suspicion" any time that individuals or organizations characterize themselves and others along the lines of nebulous and emotionally charged terms. Even when an entity tries to explain itself not only are

II: The Sociological Nature of Terrorism

≈⋊≈

lassical political sociology and critical sociology offer students of te
terrorism a wide range of concepts and perspectives that have so far el
standard security and criminal justice angles. Security and criminal ju
fine and dandy but they tend to constrict rather than expand our comprehe
terror when, combined, and in their worst (sometimes sensationalist and e
neurial) forms, they construct a paranoid and prophetically hysterical imag
world where dastardly villains are always on the brink of raining doom and des
on a hapless population of do-gooders. There certainly are bad people in the wo
would love nothing more than to harm America and its allies but, for exam
now defunct "war on terror" metaphor transformed the concrete problem of in
ist conflict into a fantasy world of good versus evil, purity versus impurity, con
versus taboo, us versus them, and victim versus perpetrator. In this chapter
briefly examine: (a) the concept of terrorism and some academic perspectives
problem and how the era of the suicide bomber beginning in the 1980s has re
ured our perceptions; (b) the critical social psychology of terror with a special e
sis on the mirrored relationship between the political–theological aspects of th
imperialist agenda and the goals of its counterimperialist reactions as well as
domestic reactions that serve to introduce our concept of sociological **hetera**
(c) ideal typical models of premodern and modern societies that will enable us to
grasp the fusion of elements within the "postmodern" world of terror, especial
concept of **piacularism**, which, in some respects, is dynamically linked and op|
to "heterarchy" as it is defined here; and (d) the relation and limits of terror wit
concepts of crime and war.

Terrorism and its Characteristic Features

Few concepts are as notoriously difficult to pin down as terror or terrorism. Our w
"terror" comes from the Latin *terrere* for "frighten," which, by itself, does not seen
offer much of a handle on things terroristic. The moral connotations of the terms s.
through time as well: "The Terror" or the "Reign of Terror" refer to phases of
French Revolution which most people in the West consider to have been a progress

we required to interpret their claims and sayings but we also have to recognize that a claim is itself the product of an interpretation and, in the case of an explanation or framing mechanism, also an attempt to justify or legitimate (Stewart 1989).

To a certain extent, terrorism is a label used for impression management and propaganda purposes. As Tilly says, "Some vivid terms serve political and normative ends admirably despite hindering description and explanation of the social phenomena at which they point. Those double-edged terms include riot, injustice, and civil society, all of them politically powerful but analytically elusive … They also include terror, terrorism, and terrorists" (2004: 5).

Terrorism is, as we see here, a *construct* and a process of authoritative interpretation (Turk 2004: 271). "Terrorist" is a label state agents use to discredit violence as nothing more than illegitimate criminal acts by gangs of individuals. "Terrorist" is also a label used to categorize those who come out on the losing side in violent struggles (Rubenstein 1987: 26–34).

The concepts of terror, terrorism, and terrorist are relative and today's terrorist may very well be transformed into tomorrow's freedom fighter and, vice versa, today's national hero may be reduced to an insurgent or criminal ringleader later on. The moral career of 19th-century abolitionist **John Brown** (here a terrorist, there a freedom fighter) has been used by many authors as an example of the contested nature of terrorism. However, the model of terrorism that developed through the seventies and eighties changed decisively after the rise of the suicide bomber in the mid-eighties and especially after 9/11.

There is nothing new about wartime suicide attacks against combatants (e.g., Kamikaze pilots during World War II) but the kind of "human bomb" we see routinely in newspapers, online, and television broadcasts was "invented" in the early eighties when combatants blew themselves up in a series of attacks during the Lebanese Civil War, the most devastating of which occurred on October 23, 1983 when the barracks at the Beirut airport were destroyed by members of Islamic *jihad* killing nearly 300 U.S. and French servicemen. Under the classic model of terrorism, actors were generally not using their bodies and selves as weapons but, now, the human being qua bomb delivery system is the weapon of choice (Zedalis 2004: 1). People are at this very moment lining up to use their bodies to destroy their enemies and this now includes a good number of women. The first female suicide bomber was 16-year-old Khyadali Sana who was responsible for killing two Israeli soldiers.

Since then, women have driven bomb-laden vehicles, carried bomber "bags," and strapped massive explosives and metal implements on their bodies in Lebanon, Sri Lanka, Chechnya, Israel, and Turkey. Terrorist groups which have publicized their use of females include the Syrian Socialist National Party (SSNP/PPS), the Liberation Tigers of Tamil Eelam (LTTE), the Kurdistan Workers Party (PKK), Chechen rebels, Al Aqsa Martyrs, Palestinian Islamic Jihad (PIJ), and, most recently, Hamas.

There are many "firsts" in this listing of organized feminine terror. While the SSNP has the distinction of deploying the first female suicide bomber, the "LTTE became the world's foremost suicide bombers and proved the tactic to be so unnerving and effective that their methods and killing innovations were studied and copied, most notably in the Middle East." The LTTE has committed the most attacks, close to 200, using women bombers in 30–40 percent. The largest number killed (170) was in Moscow in October 2002 when Chechen rebels (including a high percentage of women) held hostages in the Theater Center, and the police killed 129 captives and 41 rebels in a futile rescue effort. During the last 2 years, Palestinian suicide bombers have carried out the largest number of attacks.

(ibid.: 2)

The suicide bomber is frequently called the new "smart bomb," meaning that the bomb can "guide itself" to the target and detonate at will. The "smartness" of this new weapon has to be situated within the changing nature of the civilian target. The idea of the innocent bystander or a civilian population means less than it did prior to 9/11. From the standpoint of **Hamas**, there may be no such thing as "innocent" Jews in Israel. Likewise, during the 9/11 attacks civilians killed in the World Trade Center attacks were not seen as innocents or bystanders but as "complicitous." As Goodwin says, this kind of "categorical" terrorism bundles these victims together along with the root target because they "(1) routinely *benefit from* the actions of the government or state that the revolutionaries oppose, (2) *support* the government or state, and/or (3) have a substantial capacity to *influence* or to direct the government or state" (2006: 2,037). This was the sentiment behind Ward Churchill's infamous and ill-advised labeling of the 9/11 victims "little Eichmanns," which meant that they were "a cadre of faceless bureaucrats and technical experts who had willingly (and profitably) harnessed themselves to the task making America's genocidal world order hum with maximal efficiency" (2003: 19).

Ironically, the Bush administration's rhetorical management of the 9/11 attacks also had the effect of playing into this logic by transforming all Americans into valid targets.

"[E]very American is a soldier" now, declared George W. Bush one month after September 11, 2001. Speaking at the first meeting of the new Homeland Security Council, whose opening order of business was to beef up U.S. border operations by tightening immigration surveillance and control, Mr. Bush's pronouncement itself performed a consequential border crossing. His sweeping rhetorical induction of the entire U.S. citizenry into the ranks of military combatants obliterated the very boundary between "civilian" and "soldier" on which popular understandings of "terrorism" fundamentally depend: would future attacks on U.S. civilians now be acknowledged as a targeted assault on U.S. soldiers?

(Orr 2004: 452)

When Bush attempted to designate *all* Americans as soldiers he unwittingly took a page from the proto-Nazi Erich von Ludendorff's musings on "Total War," whereby

> [e]very individual in the nation is expected to give his entire strength either at the front or at home, and this he can only do when he realizes that it is an immutable and inviolable truth that the war is being waged solely for the existence of the nation. A totalitarian policy must put at the disposal of such a war the strength of the nation and preserve it and only a conformity to the fundamental racial and spiritual laws will succeed in welding nation, conduct of war, and politics into that powerful unity which is the basis of national preservation.
>
> (Von Lundendorff cited in Turner 1967: 150–51)

As we will see later, this rhetorical move of transforming the millions of individuals composing a plural society into a united "we" dedicated to the combating of evil terrorists is one that is designed to squelch doubt, resolve ambivalence, maximize anxiety, marginalize dissent, target internal enemies, prepare for the creation of domestic scapegoats, make **sacred** future military excursions and all sacrifices in lives, time, energy, and money that will have to be made, and, perhaps most serious, transform a multitude of self-seeking individuals into a totalized system. Implicit in the framing of the 9/11 attacks and the drive toward war in Iraq and Afghanistan was the recognition that internal or domestic psychology was as decisive as the social psychology of hijackers.

The enemy was constructed as unified, determined, and maniacal. A nation that was undisciplined, self-absorbed, and adrift could not hope to contend with such a threat. This *relationship of internal and external* is one that will recur in this book and is important. What goes on "over there" is inextricably connected with what goes on "over here." As such, when representative Paul Ryan (Republican, Wisconsin) said "it's like Cairo's moved to Madison these days," he was not far from the truth. What he was getting at was that the Egyptian phase of the **Arab Spring** that saw the toppling of Egyptian president Hosni Mubarak was dynamically linked with, and reflected back into, the imperial core, in the form of the massive protests against Wisconsin Governor Scott Walker, after he crushed the collective bargaining rights of state workers (see Mahanta 2011). Put simply: the resources, money, and energy required to expand an empire across the globe must come from somewhere and the bulk of it is extracted from the domestic population in the form of austerity and repression.

Terrorism studies have shifted primarily to the analysis of Islamic groups and the Middle East and U.S. federal law enforcement agencies have made Islamic *jihadists* their top priority—as of January 1, 2012 all but one of the Federal Bureau Investigation's (FBI's) most wanted terrorists fall into this category. What is missing is that the bad guys being fought "over there" (e.g., Iraq, Afghanistan, Pakistan, and Yemen) are "mirrored" by particular mentalities within the United States that make a war on terror possible and even desirable for many. Terrorism is not just about the bad guys but also about us. We seem to display weird similarities and even direct relations with our antagonists that might not be as superficial as they appear.

We see terrorists on television portrayed as gun-toting religious fanatics, yet America, alone among all Western nations, is literally awash in firearms and every state in the nation except for Illinois has made it legal for guns to be concealed and carried in public. When the Bush administration first attempted to pitch the "global war on terror" to the American public and international audiences it did so in the explicit terms of a "crusade" against evil and the Pentagon couched the impending holy war under the banner of Operation Infinite Justice "until they were advised that only God could dispense 'infinite justice'" (Kellner 2003: 58). Another illustration of this weird relationship between the internal and external, the us versus them polarity, lies in the training of an Iranian terrorist group in Nevada. Authorized by the Bush administration, the U.S. Joint Special Operations Command trained members of Mujahideen-e-Khalq (MEK) despite the fact that the MEK has been on the U.S. Department of State's (DOS's) list of terrorist organizations for years (Hersh 2008: 65–66). Terrorism is not just about acts perpetrated against us by others but a *relation* between us and them and this applies not only to the hardware of terror (e.g., the expanded use of drone weapons over Yemen in 2012 mirrored by the introduction of drone surveillance planes over the skies of America) but also in terms of **ideologies** and collective psychology.

When we examine the minds of terrorists we expect to find deranged maniacs or psychotics. But terrorists have struck researchers as being surprisingly "normal" when it comes to their mental states (by contrast, see Scott-Clark and Levy 2010 on teen suicide bombers). However, the idea here is not to let violent fanatics off the hook by seeing them as "normal" people just like you and me but, more disturbingly, finding within them and ourselves particular drives, desires, ideologies, and patterns of collective thought that enable us to function and participate in the world of terror. In other words, if terror and terrorism are not just disconnected, external things over and against us but somehow intimately connected to our own subjectivities, could we not locate an "inner terrorist" where we least expect to find it? Let us briefly examine the "mirror" of the terrorist and antiterrorist minds.

The Social Psychology of Terror

Antisocial personality disorders are real. Psychopaths and sociopaths exist and narcissism is also a recognized pathology but there is no diagnosis for a terrorist personality disorder and there is little evidence to shore up the belief that terrorists suffer from mental illnesses or personality disorders (Cottam et al. 2010: 270–71). Terrorists are generally not crazy. Does psychology, then, offer any insight? Sociology is more or less antipsychological because it has an aversion to reducing **social facts** to the level of one-sided subjectivity. Social facts are, if anything, objectively real or external to the individual psyche. This externality does *not* diminish in any way the subjective reality for individuals but, nonetheless, sociology can make little headway so long as it remains bogged down in the infinity of the individual psyche. Still, *political* psychology does offer some interesting insights into the social **character structure** (see Fromm and Maccoby 1996 [1970]: 16) of those who engage in political violence.

There was a good deal of work done during the eighties on the differences between right-wing (fascist, neo-Nazi, etc.) and left-wing (communist) terrorist groups in Europe with fascists drawing more from the poor and downwardly mobile working class and left-wing groups drawing more from students, professional, and technical types (Hoffman 1984; Wasmund 1986; Weinberg and Eubank 1988). From the critical perspective, however, there is really is no such thing as a truly *revolutionary* or genuinely "left-wing" form of terror. What goes by the name of "left-wing" terrorism or "revolutionary terror" is not revolutionary at all. Even when many so-called leftists fight under the banner of some radical ideology, the rhetoric of liberation and democracy is used to gloss over a pseudorevolutionary, authoritarian core. We have to remember that there is a dramatic difference between the genuine revolutionary or radical and the *rebel*.

> By rebel I refer to a person who fights existing authorities, but who himself wants to be an authority (to whom others submit), and who does not dissolve his dependence on and respect for authority per se. His rebelliousness is directed mainly against those authorities who do not acknowledge him, and he is friendly to those authorities who are of his own choosing, especially when he becomes one of them. The type of the "rebel," in this psychological sense, can be found among many radical politicians who are rebels before they have power, and turn conservative once they have acquired power for themselves. A "revolutionary" in the psychological sense is someone who overcomes his ambivalence toward authority because he frees himself from attachment to authority and from the wish to dominate others. He achieves true independence and he overcomes the yearning for domination of others.
>
> (Fromm 1959: 64)

As Zizek (2012) says, a fight may embody the "spirit of revolt without revolution" and the ostensibly revolutionary movement may, in fact, obscure an unconscious desire not for freedom but for a different form of subjugation, a different master to replace the old one. Is there no difference between "left" and "right" then? Of course there is and true revolutionaries do find themselves in organized violent resistance against tyranny and revolutionary groups may be contaminated with authoritarian personalities, but it makes better sense to set aside determinations such as "left" and "right" and look at core drivers.

When we find a group embracing a strategy of terror in the struggle for positive freedom we should be suspicious: what we see or hear on the surface may not be the decisive factor. The paradox of fighting for freedom with weapons, killing in the name of life, was one that Trotsky recognized: "our problem is not the destruction of human life, but its preservation. But as we have to struggle for the preservation of human life with arms in our hands, it leads to the destruction of human life—a puzzle the dialectical secret of which was explained by old Hegel" (2007 [1920]: 54). With all due respect to Trotsky, however, the true radical is a biophile, not a destructive necrophile, and I think Trotsky's own words betray his mostly rebellious, rather than truly radical, nature.

> As for us [Bolsheviks], we were never concerned with the Kantian-priestly and vegetarian-Quaker prattle about the "sacredness of human life". We were revolutionaries in opposition, and have remained revolutionaries in power. To make the individual sacred we must destroy the social order which crucifies him. And this problem can only be solved by blood and iron.
>
> (ibid.: 63)

It is reasonable for peace-loving people to defend themselves with force if necessary but the valorization of "blood and iron" seems to occupy another dimension altogether. Terrorists might seem on the surface to epitomize nothing less than the radical spirit of freedom and anti-authoritarianism. Yet, when we get below the surface we can locate a powerful psychic structure that helps explain the terrorist spirit: the rebellious authoritarian character linked with a plan for destructiveness aimed at illegitimate, ruling power.

Authoritarianism is the desire to submit to something or obey somebody recognized as a higher authority or legitimate power alloyed with a drive to subordinate and control groups or individuals who are weaker or perceived to be morally inferior. An orientation toward strength and weakness, submission and domination, are the essential aspects of the authoritarian personality (Adorno, et al. 1950; Altemeyer 1996; Fromm 1941; Waller 2002; Worrell 1998). However, if authoritarians are devoted to authority, why do they lash out violently at establishment authority? The key here is the idea of legitimacy (Weber cited in Gerth and Mills 1953: 195).

Domination that is held to be legitimate enjoys *authority* whereas a ruling power that is perceived to be illegitimate controls through unloved *coercion*. Authority enjoys a degree of reverence whereas simple domination bends the will through fear and might. For a better grasp of a reaction against what was believed to be illegitimate domination, we can briefly turn to the American terrorist movements of the eighties and nineties.

During the decade before 9/11 a wave of research came forward mapping a complex web of violent, conspiratorial organizations that made up a homegrown terrorist movement aimed at purifying the United States of what they considered moral and ethnic pollution as well as resisting or defeating the U.S. federal government which, for all of these groups, ruled as an alien power and represented the leading edge of a "New World Order" dominated by Jews and communists (Aho 1994; Diamond 1995; Stern 1996). The common designation for the federal government among these types was "Zionist Occupation Government" (ZOG). These anti-ZOG outfits were modern descendents of earlier hate groups such as the **Ku Klux Klan** (KKK), **Silver Shirts**, and the **Minutemen,** as well as groups that survive today like the **Posse Comitatus**. The nineties saw a rash of spectacular collisions between the state and various groups and individuals at Ruby Ridge, Idaho (1992), Waco, Texas (1993), and the Alfred P. Murrah Building in Oklahoma City (1995) fueled by a potent mixture of apocalyptic Christianity, neo-Nazism, hyper-patriotism, the spread of paramilitary survivalist cults, the flourishing of outlandish conspiracy theories, and rabid antisemitism.

According to the Anti-Defamation League, the post-1995 domestic terror landscape remains a concern but the eruptions of the nineties were successfully disorganized, contained, or pushed to the furthest fringes of society (2005). What was not eradicated, however, was the pervasive and growing sense that the state is not only fundamentally broken but has been captured by something that does not share the interests of the "average American." One has the sense that this sentiment is now even a commonplace among "mainstream" Americans and is reflected in language such as the "99 percent" versus the "one percent" and in progressive movements such as Occupy as well as corporate organized reactions such as the Tea Party. Progressives see the problem as one of money corrupting the state and the reactionaries see the problem as one of the state corrupting **capitalism** but they both, nonetheless, have problems with the state as an unresponsive, uncaring, and even hostile or alien force. The idea of unified alien power that rules with excessive coercion over a people against the interests of the greater good and universal ideals is called "sociological heterarchy" and represents the fusion of personal estrangement, social disorganization, and the experience of life as a web of inexorable traps set by self-serving and heavy-handed rulers. Seen through the lens of heterarchy, the US government appears as an analog to Durkheim's characterization of a "bourgeois administration with the gendarme to protect it" (1974: 74), where the citizenry is reduced to a "swarming of the bees" (Durkheim 1951 [1897]: 378) or a disorganized tumbling of "liquid molecules" (ibid.: 389) under the supervision of an oppressive state security apparatus—what Marx referred to as the monstrosity of a "*république cosaque*" or "Cossack republic" (1963: 119).

The American militia movements of the nineties and Palestinian suicide bombers today both have one thing in common: the absolute opposition to *established* authority (e.g., ZOG, in the case of US terrorists, and the Israeli occupation of the West Bank, Gaza Strip, and the Golan Heights in the case of Palestinians). In both cases the established ruling power is seen as illegitimate and, for justice and freedom to reign, it is necessary to destroy it or greatly reduce its power and scope. Once the status quo is overturned, however, those that had previously been denied representation and recognition will pave the way for the establishment of a new, just, and righteous rule.

This epoch of righteousness is, of course, purely imaginary and is basically a projection of the unfettered dreams of the perpetrators of violence.

Destructiveness is comprehended as qualitatively distinct and even opposed in some ways to an authoritarianism that, as we have seen, wants to symbiotically bond with a stronger power while, at the same time, crushing or subordinating an inferior (morally if not physically) object and making it dependent upon it. Destructiveness, on the other hand, seeks not to bond with and control others but to altogether eliminate sources of frustration (Fromm 1941). These two solutions to the thwarting of life in the modern world, authoritarianism and destructiveness, are distinct and in some ways mutually exclusive but at the aggregate level the two spirits may *alternate* as part of an organized strategy to overthrow a social system, may be *superimposed* on top of one another as two parallel drives, or may even *fuse* into a new form that combines rebellious authoritarian submission (to the will writ large) with destruction of enemies that stand between corrupt reality and the actualization of an imaginary world. It is important to emphasize that what is logically incompatible at the level of the individual psyche may be blended or "resolved" on a higher scale of collective belief and action. What is an *either–or* conundrum for the single person can become the logic of *both* for a movement. For the moment we can leave these various threads dangling in mid-air and pick them back up again later when we examine the human bomb. For now it is enough to note that, for the destructive authoritarian, until such time as the establishment can be overthrown, the collective mental coordinates of the suppressed group are fixed on an ideal or imaginary authority that exists outside of time and space as, for example, the "will of God" or some such thing and, after the defeat of the evil other, the imaginary power is relocated to the victorious group that imagines itself as and claims to be the carriers of the universal will (of god, the people, etc.). To put it simply, terrorists are violently opposed to authority until the day they themselves become the established authority.

This mentality of destroying what exists as a pretext for the creation of a new order (and the search for a new set of relations of obedience and command) is only half the story, however. If the United States finds itself engaged in a war against destructive authoritarian "fanatics," it would be natural to assume that a fight against terror is undertaken by peace-loving, rational lovers of democracy. This assumption would be scientifically unwarranted and what we find is that authoritarianism and destructiveness are characteristics of many Americans and their elected and unelected officials. Put simply: it seems clear that the current war on "Islamofascism" (see, e.g., Hitchens 2007) was planned and executed by different kinds of "fascists," which is a loaded way of saying that the war on terror is, in some respects, a war of violent authoritarians against a counterposed class of violent authoritarians. As Kellner puts it, "The opposing sides in the current Terror War between the Bush [and now Obama] administration reactionaries and **Al Qaeda** could be perceived as representing complementary poles of a reactionary right-wing conservatism and militarism confronted by an atavistic and premodern version of Islam and nihilistic terrorism" (2003: 22).

While liberal apologists will scoff at the idea that President Obama is a right-wing reactionary, his progressive critics will point to an unbroken continuum between his administration's prosecution of the war on terror and that of his Republican predecessor. Indeed, with regard to the "war" against transparency and accountability, President Obama is "much worse" than his predecessor.

Calling the reaction to … 9/11 … a "war" ensured that the government could justify classifying everything associated with fighting it. Under President George Bush, journalists' efforts to figure out how the United States was waging this war against al-Qaeda were often criticized by senior administration leaders, members of Congress, cable television pundits, even the public. Many of those journalists hoped that would change under … Obama. It is true the president and his cabinet members have not publically disparaged the news media as much as his predecessor did. But … President Obama's Justice Department has taken a more aggressive tack against the unauthorized disclosure of classified information by pursuing more so-called leak investigations than the Bush administration.

(Priest and Arkin 2011: xx–xxi)

Oddly enough, the more Al Qaeda is dealt one crippling blow after another on foreign battlefields the more the war against terror "out there" is shifting decisively toward rooting out imagined "extremists" *within* the borders of the United States and allied nations. And if these extremists do not exist (America, in fact, has only a superficial history of Islamic radicalism to point to) then they will have to be invented by the state. The war against "them" is simultaneously a war against "us" and our democratic principles and institutions. Are Americans primed and willing to participate in something analogous to another Red Scare where the new villain is the specter of the hidden Islamofascist in the neighborhood mosque or university study group?

There is a wide and deep body of political psychology research stretching back to the early 1950s that has convincingly shown that the American public is plagued by levels of authoritarianism that defies expectations for a nation supposedly imbued with the spirit of freedom and democracy. Even during World War II, when we as a nation were engaged in a mortal struggle with Nazis, Fascists, and Japanese totalitarians, not only were approximately 50 percent of the working class supporting the war effort on the home front antisemitic authoritarians of one degree or another but approximately 10 percent were outright Nazi sympathizers (Worrell 2008). However, I think it is also the case that the currents of authoritarianism coursing through the body politic in the America of 2001 were weaker or perhaps simply less organized than the authoritarian beliefs and emotions that drove neoconservatives and the Bush administration to war in the Middle East in the wake of September 11. Some credit has to be extended to the

American public when we consider the bold lies, deception, and a torrent of unceasing propaganda (on the part of the state and corporate media) regarding weapons of mass destruction and links to terror designed to gain support for a preemptive attack on a nation that posed no threat to American security.

Much has been made of the connection between the Nazi legal philosopher Carl Schmitt and the contemporary neoconservative movement in the United States. It is probably not the case that Bush, Cheney, and their ideological brethren were taking their cues directly from Schmitt's writings, but it is the case that both **neoconservativism** and Schmitt's brand of **political theology** are exemplary models of political authoritarianism and cut from the same philosophical cloth.

One of the hallmarks of political theology is the idea that exceptional historical moments (e.g., the post-World War I crisis in Germany or the post-9/11 situation in the United States) require a suspension of norms, e.g., curtailment of civil liberties and other deprivations and necessary sacrifices, and that the executive (the President) is justified in exercising what amounts to dictatorial and unconstitutional powers. In short, exceptional moments make necessary actions that may even be unlawful (torture, suspension of *habeas corpus,* secret overseas prisons, the assassination of American citizens suspected of terrorism without a trial, and so on). We saw a massive increase, additionally, in the use of "signing statements" during the Bush years. The American Bar Association

> determined that signing statements that signal the president's intent to disregard laws adopted by Congress undermine the separation of powers by depriving Congress of the opportunity to override a veto, and by shutting off policy debate between the two branches of government. According to the task force, they operate as a "line item veto," which the U.S. Supreme Court has ruled unconstitutional.
>
> (American Bar Association 2006)

Moreover, once a power has become institutionalized like this, executive successors do not relinquish them voluntarily. The attacks on September 11 were constructed by the White House and the cooperative mass media as the dawning of a new era in American geopolitics: after 9/11 "many public officials and commentators were quick to declare that a different kind of 'new world' had come into being, a world of fears where 'barbarians' were turning sophisticated technologies against the advanced civilization that had invented them" (Wolin 2008: 69–70).

Another hallmark of political theology is the dividing of the world and nations into friends versus enemies that must engage in mortal combat in order for the strong to achieve its rightful place as political master. Bush's appeal to Americans and the world to assist in the war on terror spelled out just this kind of dualism: either you are with us or you are for the terrorists. The world was now split along these two and only these two lines. Whether you wanted to be on one side or another or neither was irrelevant. You were either going to support a war or you were stigmatized as a virtual terrorist yourself. You were either anti-evil or evil. Who wants to be seen weighing the pros and cons of evil? Wait and see was not an option. Critical analysis, discussion, and deliberation were all defunct impulses. This was just the kind of resurgent binary opposition that some in the US had been waiting for since the early nineties.

When the Soviet Union fell apart and the Cold War ended in 1991, the United States faced a scenario of unrivaled military superiority and world dominance. In some respects, this was a disaster for conservatives of various stripes because they had lost the ruthless, global bogeyman that gave meaning to the American project of anticommunism that shaped foreign and domestic policy from the end of World War II. In other words, many people based their personal, religious, and political identities on the existence and future defeat of the Soviet Union and it was suddenly gone. This could not be a victory for those that engage in "definition by repudiation" (Slotkin 1973: 22) or knowing what you are by what you are not. The philosopher Leonard Nelson once put it like this: the good is the evil we choose to ignore (1957 [1917]: 90) and when you lose the evil or the self-defining negative, history has effectively ended.

Normal, ordinary people looked forward to a new day of diminished defense spending, reinvestment in domestic life, and fewer foreign entanglements. Empire, though, must expand if it is to survive (Neumann 1944: 33). During World War II, the sociologist Robert Park noted, "There must always be some great collective enterprise on the national agenda in which all classes can actively participate .... War has been and still is the greatest, the most strenuous ... enterprise in which nations can engage" (cited in Turner 1967: 163) and some ultra right-wingers openly dreamed not of a new era of peaceful, limited prosperity but of a new Pearl Harbor (i.e., some dramatic, sudden, and catastrophic event) that would give the United States an excuse to unleash its military might and reshape the globe to best suit American imperial interests.

[A] 2000 report circulated titled "Rebuilding American Defense: Strategies, Forces and Resources for A New American Century." Drawn up by the neoconservative think tank Project for a New American Century (PANC) for a group that ... [at the time included] [Vice President Dick] Cheney, [Secretary of Defense Donald] Rumsfeld, and [Deputy Secretary of Defense] Paul Wolfowitz, the document spelled out a plan for US world hegemony grounded in US military dominance ... and control of the Persian Gulf region with its oil supplies. Its upfront goals were "Pax Americana" and US domination of the world during the new millennium.

(Kellner 2003: 21; bold added; see glossary)

The deadly attacks on 9/11 provided the "neocons" just the pretext they dreamed of for inaugurating the new age of "Pax Americana." Terrorism was latched on to even before the Union of Soviet Socialist Republics (USSR) vanished in a puff of smoke as a potential threat that could legitimate a more-of-the-same posture that would continue to plow trillions of dollars into the military industrial complex, augment the state security apparatus, and demand further austerity for Americans and subjugated nations in order to fund yet another wave of military adventurism. Terror had an "upside" to it compared with conventional military adversaries: the shadowy enemy could be constructed to appear "weak enough to be attacked with impunity but sufficiently threatening to mobilize the general population in support of the [Reagan administration's] expansion of state power at home and violence abroad" (Chomsky 1989: 269). Unlike national powers, terrorist groups are pitifully weak in comparison. Yes, 9/11 and its military aftermath was bloody, but compared with conventional conflicts the war on terror is relatively "risk free" for the state to engage in.

If the USSR was too powerful to attack directly without the very real danger of mutual annihilation and if the USSR's proxy states (Korea and Vietnam) proved to be too much for the United States to handle then terror was something that could be managed profitably. Al Qaeda may be dangerous but there is no Al Qaeda navy or air force, they have no Marines, nor an army of one million well-trained soldiers. Al Qaeda has no armored divisions, air cavalry, artillery brigades, stealth bombers, carrier battle groups, rotor and fixed wing assets, submarine fleets, drone squadrons, or intercontinental ballistic missiles, and it certainly lacks satellite surveillance and space-based systems. Where terrorists manage to blow up a disco here, a barracks there, an aircraft, an embassy, or even multiple buildings, the USSR, in contrast, could have reduced much of the planet to smoldering ash in a few minutes.

It would be an exaggeration to portray Al Qaeda as nothing more than a ragtag band of cave-dwelling misfits, but that caricature comes far closer to the truth than how Al Qaeda and other terrorist groups have been built up by corporate media and the state. In a nutshell, *America has finally found a war it cannot lose because neither winning nor losing are possible outcomes.* In a now-infamous 2003 "war on terror memo," Donald Rumsfeld, then Secretary of Defense, admitted that there were not even "metrics" in existence that would allow for the measuring of winning or losing. "Are we capturing, killing, or deterring and dissuading more terrorists every day than the madrassas [*sic*] and the radical clerics are recruiting, training and deploying against us?" (cited in Joyner 2012). A war without "metrics" is a war with infinity, the abyss of the unknown.

Terror is the perfect spectral foe because the weaker it is the more mighty it becomes; the more remote the threat the closer it is; and the longer nothing happens the more imminent the disaster. Americans must be permanently vigilant because the emergency is permanent. To question the war on terror represents a lack of unity and antipatriotism; it is also a sign of collective weakness and weakness is not merely contemptible but invites more harm. Donald Rumsfeld's "Rules of Life" included the statement that "Weakness is provocative" (cited in Wolin 2008: 69). A more authoritarian sentiment would be difficult to find (Stone, Lederer and Christie 1993). The underlying essence of authoritarianism is that the world is divided between only those that are strong and will rule and those are that are weak and shall be dominated. Few are qualified to rule and make decisions and decisions should take the form of a univocal command.

Bush labeling himself "The Decider" made for great comedy but the underlying assumption was no laughing matter and is also a defining feature of political theology. The ideology hidden in the name "The Decider" is that of *decisionism*: "the demand for action instead of deliberation, for decision instead of evaluation" (Neumann 1944: 45). Decisionism (a) transforms all social relations into political relations and qualifies all relations for mortal combat; (b) consolidates power in the office of the executive; (c) demands unified action over worthless debate; (d) wills the submission of the press and media to the wishes of the executive; and, among other things, (e) turns earthly matters into a sublime mission.

Going right to the heart of political theology, the war on terror was made a sacred undertaking. To grasp US foreign policy we have to look no further than geopolitics and energy strategies, but to sell a war on terror to the American public we have to see how a religious logic was used to frame and sell the undertaking. Recall that the war on terror was pitched as a transcendental battle between good and evil, against an "Axis of Evil" and "evildoers." Evil is not a political concept (Kellner 2003: 61); rather, it is a highly nebulous theological notion designed not to rationally comprehend reality but to mystify the situation, repress questions and criticism, and mobilize the masses of ordinary people. "The very term 'evil' is highly archaic and has a mystifying, supernatural quality that exaggerates the power of the perpetrator so designated" (ibid.).

Unfortunately, the notion of what we might call "primitive modernism" is one that many social scientists have drawn out with regards to the emotional and intellectual irrationality of people living in the age of reason and skepticism. It is good to know something about the premodern, elementary prototypes upon which rest some of our institutions. In what follows we will have to be unjust toward the complexity of history and speak in ideal typical forms, i.e., we will construct simplified and compact models of premodern and modern societies that are exaggerated and slanted in ways that distort reality but, in so doing, draw differences out in bold relief.

Terror: Premodern, Modern, and Postmodern Fusions

Premodern social organization revolved around the clan as the basic elements of a tribe (and larger tribal confederacies). This form of segmented organization was simultaneously flexible in its simplicity but also fragile in that tribes broke apart rather easily. Social control and regulation were harsh (bordering on **fatalism**) and alternated between tradition and elder rule in times of peace and charismatic ecstasy in times of conflict. The people that constituted these clans were *members* rather than individuals. Simple and bare affluence (Sahlins 1972: 1–5), rudimentary divisions of labor,

the concepts of "*jihad*" (holy war) and "martyrdom," which enables the suicide victim to traverse the taboo of self-destruction (see Strenski 2006: 270–80).

The martyr, we are told, is in love with the sacred. "They were trying not to avoid life but to fulfill it in what they considered to be an act of both personal and social redemption. In this way they were connecting a contemporary political strategy to a sacred history of martyrdom and sacrifice" (Juergensmeyer 2008: 417). McCauley and Moskalenko reach similar conclusions: while this life may be misery the suicide is not against this life but "for god" and martyrdom transforms suffering into redemption (2011: 173, 181). The "very presence" of the martyr "is a reminder to others that there is more they can do to serve the people" (ibid.: 177) and god. The martyr also "raises the bar" of ascetic self-renunciation that impels others to measure their conduct against the higher standards of the fighter willing to give all (ibid.: 179, 185). Interestingly, suicide also raises the "value" of death and imputes a tinge of shame to the remainders who do not give "*the last full measure of devotion*" (ibid.: 184; italics in original). When one feels shamed by not "going all the way" one has a tendency to be more submissive and deferential to others who represent full devotion and hate the "evil other" that much more (we should note, here, the connection between martyrdom and authoritarian submission and the desire to destroy the hated other discussed earlier). We find that the martyr's suicide is only an extreme manifestation of a general phenomenon: the foundations of collective life upon the bedrock of self-sacrifice. Is not Western Christendom as a totality founded on an act of suicide? (Dingley 2010: 61).

When we examine the suicide bomber and the transformation of suicide into "martyrdom" we are still skirting an important element. We gain access to another dimension of reality when we recast the suicide–martyrdom problem under the concept of sacrifice, a term that we saw Durkheim use in his description of the altruistic type of suicide. Juergensmeyer does a good job in making this connection.

> This dimension of martyrdom links it to the activity that some scholars see as the most fundamental form of religiosity: sacrifice, a rite of destruction that is found in virtually every religious tradition in the world. The term suggests that the very process of destroying is spiritual since the word comes from the Latin, *sacrificium*, "to make holy." What makes sacrifice so riveting is not just that it involves killing but that it is also, in an ironic way, ennobling. The destruction is performed within a religious context that transforms the killing into something positive.
> (Juergensmeyer 2008: 417–18; see also Strenski 2006: 271–74)

There are innumerable forms of sacrifice and classificatory schemes for organizing sacrificial practices. In their classic study of sacrifice, Hubert and Mauss explored the dimensions of objective and subjective sacrifices, rites of attribution and utilization, and sacralization and **expiation** (1964 [1898]), but Durkheim's later analysis of piacular rites (1995 [1912]) takes us in a direction that will explain much of what we see in the human bomb.

"Piaculum" is derived from the Latin for expiation and appeasement but the contemporary sociological meaning goes beyond expiation. As Durkheim says, "Any misfortune, anything that is ominous, and anything that motivates feelings of disquiet or fear requires a piaculum and is therefore called piacular" (ibid.: 392–93). Piacular rites and acts are those engaged in when a group feels itself to be the victim of misfortune, in the grip of some disaster, is distressed, or is terrified. Historically we can find groups that resigned themselves to the fact that misfortune and disaster would be visited upon them by virtue of their god's vengefulness, especially when their god was already known as "a god of natural catastrophes who could and often did send pestilence and frightful misfortunes of all sorts against those who evoked this wrath" (Weber 1952: 301), but these cases are rare and popular sentiments run in the direction of the piacular rather than patient resignation.

By reframing suicide bombings under the concept of piacularism we can unify the salient features of the phenomenon and preserve its perspectival quality at the same time. In short, piacularism allows us to account for the bomber representing a case of suicide–murder from the standpoint of victims and targets while also analytically respecting the standpoint of the perpetrator that the bombing is not a suicide (which is taboo) but an act of sacrifice in a holy war. Terry Godlove (2005: 45) points to the piacular rites that characterized post-9/11 America (how we mourned as victims) and we know that some currents of reactionary pseudoconservatism in the United States are characterized by piacularism (Worrell 1999), but we should also be examining the "other side" of the terror–victim relation whereby self-annihilation and mass violence are imagined as the most appropriate solution to acute anomic crises.

Instead of being stuck with a bunch of contradictory or partial notions that cancel one another out or fail to "add up" to anything, e.g., bombings as suicide, murder, sacrifice, expiation, a gift to god, jihad, **ascetic** *self-renunciation, altruism, us, them, internal, external, politics, religion, victim, perpetrator, retribution, scapegoats, rebelliousness, radicalism, fanaticism, etc., we can reconcile their different aspects and partial truths into a unity, the product of which is a theoretical optic that is greater than and different from the sum of its parts. We will make the most headway by elevating the terms of the debate into the concept of the piacular.*

The piacular act or ritual is capable of transforming a group of ordinary people into a frenzied monstrosity and the ordinary individual into an instrument of divine fury. Punishment may be directed internally or externally. The *internal* piaculum is simply the mourning and sorrow expressed by the group and the rites of expiation for sins they feel they have committed. It would be difficult to find a group that did not, at least ever so slightly, blame themselves or engage in self-incrimination for a misfortune that has befallen them—recall that in the wake of the 9/11 attacks Jerry Falwell and Pat Robertson heaped blame for the attacks not only on the terrorists themselves but also on the sinfulness of America, as if the terrorists were instruments of divine retribution (Goodstein 2001). If nothing else, piacularism directed inward functions to firm up resolve and the sense of hardship and sacrifice that will be necessary to meet present challenges. *External* piacularism is the construction of the diabolical other that must be punished or subjected to violence as a price to be paid for inflicting misfortune and misery on the group; they turn to violence as a technique for "remedying this evil" that has befallen them (Durkheim 1995 [1912]: 407). The "evil" object will have to die. By definition, there must exist an evil X that mixes a kernel of empirical reality with myth in order to transfer blame for collective misfortune.

Once calamity hits a society it will:

> find a victim at all costs on whom the collective sorrow and anger can be discharged. This victim will naturally be sought outside, for an outsider is a subject *minoris resistentiae* [less able to resist] since he is not protected by the fellow-feeling that attaches to a relative or a neighbor, nothing about him blocks and neutralizes the bad and destructive feelings …
>
> (ibid.: 404)

Durkheim noted that in the 19th century, Jews functioned as a scapegoat in a malaise-stricken France and his remarks on French antisemitism are highly relevant (thanks to Karen Fields for making the connection between piacularism and antisemitism).

> When society undergoes suffering, it feels the need to find someone whom it can hold responsible for its sickness, on whom it can avenge its misfortunes: and those against whom public opinion already discriminates are naturally designated for this role. These are the pariahs who serve as expiatory victims. What confirms me in this interpretation is the way in which the result of **Dreyfus**'s trial was greeted in 1894. There was a surge of joy on the boulevards. People celebrated as a triumph what should have been a cause of public mourning. At last they knew whom to blame for the economic troubles and moral distress in which they lived. The trouble came from the Jews. The charge had been officially proved. By this very fact alone, things already seemed to be getting better and people felt consoled.
>
> (Durkheim cited in Lukes 1973: 345; bold added; see glossary)

Importantly, self-negation of this piacular form can be of a *partial* variety where we see people merely inconveniencing themselves or wounding themselves. More extreme, piacularism can be carried to a higher pitch where the self-negation is *total* rather than partial. Here, with total piacularism, we find the person sacrificing their life (in its entirety) in one moment. Why do people feel duty-bound to kill themselves for some higher cause or, negatively, to rid their society of some impurity? To allow society to suffer without reaction would be to display indifference and, ultimately, would signal the worthlessness or irrelevance of that society.

> If society permitted them to remain indifferent to the blow that strikes and diminishes it, it would be proclaiming that it does not hold its rightful place in their hearts. Indeed, it would deny itself. For a family [for example] to tolerate that one of its members should die without being mourned would give witness thereby that it lacks moral unity and cohesiveness. It abdicates; it renounces its existence. For his part, when the individual feels firmly attached to the society to which he belongs, he feels morally bound to share in its grief and its joy. To abandon it would be to break the ties that bind him to the collectivity, to give up wanting collectivity, and to contradict himself.
>
> (Durkheim 1995 [1912]: 403)

To sum up, the sociological concept that best captures the deeds of the human bomber is that of the total piacular rite. We must remember that the piacular act is oriented (a) toward the sacred collective representation (i.e., god) and is, therefore, a gift to god/society (see Strenski 2006 on this aspect) and is therefore an act of communion with the "positive" universal other (i.e., the group's own representation of itself); (b) the act rewards the ego and transforms the living person into a sacred symbol (the sanctified name lives on in symbolic form and circulates throughout the community's network of discourse); (c) the act firms up the survivor's sense of obligation toward enhanced self-negation (**asceticism**) and commitment to the greater cause—another view on this is that the act functions to purify the moral condition of the surviving community and counteract the sin of egoism and indifference toward the plight of the collectivity; and (d) it is a criminal act of mass murder whereby the negative universal community (i.e., the hated other blamed for the misfortunes of the suffering group) is punished.

Between Crime and War and "State Terror"

Rubenstein (1987) situates terrorism between the concepts of crime and war. Terrorists definitely engage in war-like actions, yet when we wage war against "terror" it is not against this or that state but against the concept of terror itself, which, as if magically, chooses its own human instruments; we may defeat this or that group but the spirit of terror will assuredly possess other groups. Terrorists also clearly engage in criminal actions yet we also clearly do not lump terrorism in with other simple criminal acts. Here, we can juxtapose terrorist aims and methods as well as separating the notions of terror and terrorism proper.

Take, for example, a criminal gang that assassinates or kidnaps police, judges, or military personnel as a form of intimidation for the purposes of market penetration or wealth augmentation. Some researchers would classify this kind of gang as terrorist ("narco-terrorism"). Clearly, the methods are terroristic but their aims or motivations fall short of promoting a common political agenda and the notion of fighting for or representing some particular and repressed segment of the population seems problematic. Think of it this way: who would classify a murderous drug cartel as a band of "freedom fighters"? However, keeping crime and terror separate as "ideal types" projects clarity into what is, in reality, a murky situation; terror may fund itself by engaging in operations that are purely criminal and terrorist units may "devolve" into purely criminal gangs (Adams 1986). And if motivations are important then how are we to evaluate them? Some would argue that motivations should be set aside as unknowable and just focus on external effects, yet doing so is tantamount to a positivistic flushing away of sociologically decisive concerns for things like "moral currents" and non-material (but nonetheless objectively real) social forces. The lure of "positive" science and its goal to "understand" is to reduce terrorism to precisely measurable variables but the road to sociological comprehension is a negative one where few things present themselves as a solid, measurable crystal. Just as the boundaries between terrorism and crime are troublesome so are those that separate terrorism and warfare.

War is defined as sustained armed conflict between societies resulting in large-scale loss of life or extreme material destruction. Engaging in war either directly or indirectly though a proxy is one of the principal means through which a society, **status group**, political party, or social class projects force for the purpose of increasing economic, political, or geographic strength, weakening a rival, or pacifying some real or perceived threat (Worrell 2011). We do not normally associate terrorism with a whole society, a status group, a party, or an entire class of people. Some parties have identifiable terrorist wings but the parties themselves usually attempt to strenuously separate the party itself from any violent rump such that the party retains a degree of legitimacy vis-à-vis the state that it is in opposition to. For example, the Muslim Brotherhood is neither a terrorist organization nor is it a political party per se (it is a large and durable social–religious movement with millions of members), but it has spawned political parties and there have been terrorist groups emerging from or attached to these parties. The line of demarcation between a party and a terrorist organization is often amorphous and subject to change (Weinberg 1991).

If a state, however, designates the whole party as nothing more than a terrorist organization lacking all legitimacy and then wages a military campaign against this group then terrorism shades off into war and, paradoxically, the act of waging war transforms the "terrorist" into something greater than and different from a terrorist. Think of it like this: the state does not wage war against terrorists because they have formed a party; rather, they are a "party" because the state wages war against it. Sociologically, we see here the transformative effect of ideological inversion. For example, according to Durkheim, we do not punish an individual or group because they are criminals; rather, they are "criminals" because we punish them (1984 [1893]: 31–39). In an important respect declaring war against terrorists plays directly into their goals: elevating the particular into a recognized universal on the same conceptual plane as the state, in other words, converting the terrorist (illegitimate) into a legitimate political entity recognized by the state. This leads to the problem of state terror.

Can a state or government wage a terrorist campaign? This is unclear and a matter of longstanding debate that we cannot resolve here. Take, for example, the Nazi genocide during World War II. Clearly, the mass murders perpetrated in concentration camps were horrifying and terrorist methods were used, but were Nazis "terrorists" in the sociological sense? Again, who would classify Nazis under the rubric of "freedom fighters"? We can see why the alternative of "freedom fighters" would be terribly offensive if we cannot instead fit Nazis under a rubric of terror. Terrorism proper implicates a particularity or identifiable group (even if negatively identified) that stands in opposition to some universal power. Rather than answering the question of state terror once and for all we will have an opportunity to reflect further on the question later.

DISCUSSION QUESTIONS

1. Why is terrorism so difficult to define?
2. Are terrorists radicals or are they reactionaries?
3. Should Americans be at all concerned about their collective political psychology when, measured by their own standards, terrorists are seen as normal?
4. How can the concepts of authoritarianism, destructiveness, and anomie help us understand the intellectual and emotional "climate" in a world of terror and counterterror?
5. How does the concept of piacularism help to make sense of the human bomber?

III: The War on Terror
and the Business of Security

~~~><~~~

The phrase "global war on terror" has fallen out of favor with politicians lately, but as Joyner (2012) points out, the Obama administration, "through its amplified use of drones, escalated and expanded that war in all but name". Indeed, this war, already more than a decade old, may run on indefinitely. As Zakaria says, "it is increasingly clear that the United States is winding down its massive military commitments to the two wars of the last decade. We are out of Iraq and we will soon be largely out of Afghanistan. **Osama bin Laden** is dead, and Al Qaeda is a shadow of its former self. Threats remain but these are being handled using special forces and intelligence. So, finally, after a decade we seem to be right-sizing the threat from terrorist groups. Or are we?"

> While we will leave the battlefields of the greater Middle East, we are firmly committed to the war on terror at home .... Since September 11, 2001, the US government has created or reconfigured at least 263 organizations to tackle some aspect of the war on terror. Thirty-three new building complexes have been built for the intelligence bureaucracies alone, occupying 17 million square feet—the equivalent of 22 US Capitols or three Pentagons. The largest bureaucracy after the Pentagon and Department of Veteran Affairs is now the Department of Homeland Security which has a workforce of 230,000 people.
>
> (Zaharia 2012)

Since the turn of the 20th century, the United States has developed a dependency on military conflict and war. Excluding clashes within its own borders (e.g., the Civil War or the genocide of indigenous populations), the Congressional Research Service reports that the United States has been involved in well over 300 wars, armed conflicts, skirmishes, and various forms of military engagement between 1798 and 2009 (Grimmett 2010). The number of actual shooting wars and battles is around 130 (Worrell 2011: 2). The name "America" is virtually synonymous with war and when we want to solve a social problem, poverty for example, we wage a "war" on it. The same goes for illegal drugs and terror. And how about medical problems like Alzheimer's disease? We "combat" them. Why do we wage "war" (literally and rhetorically) when we want to solve a problem and why do we wage wars on abstractions? Why is the bad other always a combatant? One reason is that wars (physical and virtual) are economically and politically profitable for corporations and the **power elite** in general.

When I was in the Marines we used to sing songs about Smedley Butler, twice a recipient of the Congressional Medal of Honor and, arguably, the most famous Marine in history. Little did I know that Butler's own views on the function of the military were quite at odds with the myths propagated by my drill instructors.

> "I helped make Mexico … safe for American oil interests in 1914. I helped make Haiti and Cuba a decent place for the National City Bank boys to collect revenues in. I helped in the raping of half a dozen Central American republics for the benefits of Wall Street. The record of racketeering is long. I helped purify Nicaragua for the internal banking house of Brown Brothers in 1909–1912. I brought light to the Dominican Republic for American sugar interests in 1916. In China I helped to see to it that Standard Oil went its way unmolested."
>
> (Butler 2003: 10)

The vast majority of people I knew in the Marines were simply looking for an alternative to unemployment. The farm crisis of the eighties had laid waste to many plans and joining the military was a preferable route to food stamps, college, or the state penitentiary. Rulers have from time immemorial used war as a form of eugenics to dispose of surplus population and even wars ostensibly fought in the defense of the highest national ideals are, in their own ways, eugenics programs (see Fussell 1996: 172 for his experiences in World War II). The military is an institution that soaks up young males (and a few women) that would otherwise fall between the cracks and puts them to work as leg-breakers for industry and finance. Of course, *voluntary self-incarceration* sounds incredibly cynical so an inordinate amount of ritual sacralization and eyewash is directed at mystifying military service. Being an expendable tool and corporate thug from General Butler's angle is transformed into "service to your country" and crusader against evildoers.

The War on Terror

The state is primarily responsible for solving terrorism and the state is, if anything, good at one thing above all others and that is destroying things that impede its goals. By framing terror as a "war" it lends the notion that terror is concretely real and can be defeated through military and police techniques and resources and, incidentally, lends justification to the claims that we need to dedicate ever greater sums of money on military and police budgets. The war metaphor also enables the state to operate at a level that it is most comfortable with, namely, other states. If terrorism involves a war then behind terrorists must hide the nefarious intentions of another state that sponsors terrorists as surrogate fighters (Crenshaw 1995: 10). The concept of a "war" means that there is some kind of magic formula or generic protocol for responding to all acts of terror. While the US is spectacularly good at physical destruction and mass killing it nonetheless has great difficulty in actually "winning" wars. The so-called war on terror, for example, was and continues to look like a spectacular failure. As Altemeyer says,

> Using military power in Iraq to "get Saddam" produced, not a shining democracy, but a lot of dead Americans, at least fifty times as many dead Iraqis, and the predicted civil war. The "war on terrorism" backfired considerably, as enraged Muslims around the world, with little or no connection to al Qaeda, formed their own "home-grown" terrorist cells bent on suicide attacks—especially after news of American atrocities in Iraq raced around the globe. Occupying Iraq tied down most of America's mobile ground forces, preventing their use against the resurgent **Taliban** in Afghanistan which had supported the 9/11 attacks, and making American troops easy targets in the kind of guerilla warfare that produces revenge-driven massacres within even elite units.
> (Altemeyer 2006: 190; bold added; see glossary)

This notion that the war on terror is a failure assumes, however, that it is just another war like World War II or Korea where the nemesis was in some respects concrete and measurable. Body bags contained "the bad guys" and abstractions were conjured up around an objective, material core. In the current war, however, it is abstraction first and material reality that is "fit" around a mystical core. Post-9/11, "[i]n the words of the president and the secretary of state, terror, terrorism, and terrorists become inseparable concepts, coherent entities, efficacious actors, and enemies to be eradicated" (Tilly 2004: 5). Terror, already nebulous, became a pure abstraction and an instrument used for domestic control and an emotional nebula in which the state could work to erode and dismantle civil liberties. Instead of focusing on the concrete problem the war on terror became a chimera used to erect the foundations of a massive police state and expanding empire on the shaky ground of pervasive fear and paranoia (see Brzezinski 2007).

The United States is no longer merely a country, nation, or state. The United States is an empire and empires represent a complex network of nations, alliances, threats, coercion, laws, treaties, resources, and energy and information currents. But we can simplify the system by distinguishing between the internal (core) of the system and its external (peripheral) elements. The core and peripheries are dynamically linked such that what happens on the periphery "reflects" back into the core and what happens in the core "reflects" into the periphery—recall the Mubarak–Walker image earlier. This mirror relation is true for all contested relations, but there is a difference between, say, the image of the GI battling Nazis on the battlefields of Europe and the shadows and abstractions of a war on terror. The war against empirically real fascists was one where abstractions and propaganda were woven around a material core but in the war on terror, it is the exact opposite: fragments of empirical reality are projected into the abyss of abstractions.

Despite surface appearances, terror attacks are not primarily about killing people for the sake of killing. Your chances of being killed by terrorists in the United States are certainly greater than being attacked by a crocodile and a polar bear at the same time but far less than you might have been led to believe. Let us try to put death by terrorist into perspective. According to the Centers for Disease Control and Prevention (CDC 2009) the number one killer of Americans is heart disease, which, in 2009, took the lives of 599,413 individuals, followed closely by cancer, which claimed 567,628. In other words, smoking and a poor diet are your worst enemies. Accidents ("unintentional injuries") accounted for 118,021 deaths; suicide victims numbered 36,909; and homicides resulted in the deaths of 18,309 in 2007 (CDC 2011). By comparison, *the total number of Americans killed by terrorists between 1971 and 2007* was 2,347 according to the START center at the University of Maryland (2007). Averaged over 36 years that comes to approximately 65 deaths per year. And this figure is somewhat misleading because of the number of casualties as a result of the attacks occurring on 9/11. For example, from 1997 to 2000 a total of *four* were victims of terrorism (Dean 2006: 174). What the vast majority of Americans do not realize is that terrorism consists almost entirely of Sunni extremists killing other Muslims in Islamic countries (The National Counterterrorism Center 2012: 14) and that, as far as American citizens are concerned, they should be more concerned about being killed by their own television sets and home furnishings (Zenko 2012).

Death by terrorist, *over the span of two generations*, is so improbably remote that it is not worth worrying about. Your chances of being killed by an asteroid strike, according to Ronald Bailey (2006), is a lifetime risk of about one in 200,000, compared with the chances of dying at the hands of terrorists of one in a million (that is, *if terrorists were blowing up one shopping mall in America per week*, and, of course, nothing like that is happening or will ever happen). Bailey also states that in the ten years from the 9/11 attacks to 2011, "arguably", 16 people were killed in the US as a result of terrorism: 16 deaths out of a population that is now roughly 320 million. One has to wonder, then, if "terrorism" is anything more than a myth invented by politicians and academics. But if terrorism does not represent a realistic threat to our bodily existence the same cannot be said of its impact on our way of life. *Terrorism is largely a myth and yet still a powerful social fact* that means terrorism threatens the United States but not in the way that we imagine.

What represents the real threat if not that of being killed by a terrorist in a random attack? As John Dean says, "our own government terrorizes us so much that we are willing to give up the ideals of democracy in exchange for reducing our fear" (2006: 175).

"[T]he real danger posed by terrorism for our democracy is not that they can defeat us with physical or military force," rather, "terrorism presents its real threat in provoking democratic regimes to embrace and employing authoritarian measures that

(1) weaken the fabric of democracy; (2) discredit the government domestically as well as internationally; (3) alienate segments of the population from their government, thereby pushing more people to support (passively, if not outright actively) the terrorist organizations and their causes; and (4) undermine the government's claim to the moral high ground in the battle against the terrorists, while gaining legitimacy for the latter."

(ibid.: 175–76)

Our own state uses partially real and greatly manufactured fear of terrorism as a form of social control and containment. We see here again that important connection or dynamic relationship between the external and the internal. Our frankly violent and heavy-handed foreign policies "blowback" (Johnson 2004) or reflect back into the core system in a transfigured form: the form of internal repression and the curtailment of civil liberties, the crushing of unions and the principles of collective bargaining and wage stagnation. "We" drop the metaphorical hammer on "them" who live somewhere "over there," and in so doing we have another hammer dropped on us by our own officials and institutions as part of the "shared sacrifices" needed to defeat evil. The trick is to get us to voluntarily cooperate (even perhaps enthusiastically) in our own self-defeat. But why would a democratic government have any interest in doing this to its own people? We would first have to question the extent to which we have a democratic government or even live in a democratic society.

Some commentators, e.g., Chris Hedges, see actual **fascism** rising up in America in twisted forms of evangelical Christianity pandered to by Republicans. In this scenario oily salespeople peddling eternal salvation dupe the downtrodden plebeians of Middle America, wrecked by two generations of post-industrialism, into backing reactionary politicians who promise to make the wicked pay (Hedges 2006). In short, unregulated capitalism produces hell on earth and the solution is paradoxically not the dismantling of capitalism itself but a combination of expiation for sinful living and the punishment of the perverse other (their list of infidels and devils in the United States is extensive) that has brought god's wrath on the nation. What is needed, they think, is more god and fewer gays; more bibles and less science; more vengeance and less forgiveness; and more belief and less reasoning. The United States can only devolve into an authoritarian nightmare if its citizens, on the whole, allow it to happen and Hedge's argument should make us pause to consider the deep reservoirs of social sadomasochism and destructiveness percolating in the belly of America. My own, admittedly non-empirical grasp of the situation, is that a phenomenon such as **Dominionism** is highly contradictory and to a great extent exploited for purely business purposes by wealth-oriented preachers and pandered to by flexible politicians looking for votes and campaign donations. Nonetheless, it is obvious that millions of Americans care not a whit for democracy and would gladly exchange it for an authoritarian theocracy.

For Sheldon Wolin the United States is *not* a fascist state in a historical sense but exhibits tendencies that put it on course for a new kind of totalitarianism he calls "inverted." Inverted totalitarianism is different from earlier, classical forms of totalitarianism of the types found in Nazi German and Fascist Italy. Inverted totalitarianism is characterized by: (a) rule not by charismatic leaders but by abstract (heteronomous) forces managed by executives; (b) corporate control over state functions whereby policies are subordinated entirely to corporate and business interests; (c) the replacement of government-issued propaganda with corporate control of media and the interlocking cooperation of media and corporate government such that the media parrot the official line; (d) mass apathy and political inaction on the part of the consumer-citizens; (e) hyperactive militarism and serial misadventures around the globe—one of the curious aspects of repeated U.S. military failures since World War II (Korea, Vietnam, Iraq, Afghanistan) is that ruin actually encourages further rounds of misadventure rather than sober assessments and restraint; (f) slashing budgets for social programs while simultaneously intruding into "the most personal of affairs: sexual relations, marriage, reproduction, and family decisions about life and death;" and (7) a form of democracy he calls "managed" in that everything done by the state or politicians, even the most anti-democratic, are all in the name of democracy and where "governments are legitimated by elections that they have learned to control" (2008: 41–47).

Representative institutions no longer represent voters. Instead, they have been short-circuited, steadily corrupted by an institutionalized system of bribery that renders them responsive to powerful interest groups whose constituencies are the major corporations and wealthiest Americans. The courts, in turn, when they are not increasingly handmaidens of corporate power, are consistently deferential to the claims of national security. Elections have become heavily subsidized non-events that typically attract at best merely half of an electorate whose information about foreign and domestic politics is filtered through corporate-dominated media. Citizens are manipulated into a nervous state by the media's reports of rampant crime and terrorist networks, by thinly veiled threats of the Attorney General and by their own fears about unemployment. What is crucially important here is not only the expansion of governmental power but the inevitable discrediting of constitutional limitations and institutional processes that discourages the citizenry and leaves them politically apathetic …. Thus the elements are in place: a weak legislative body, a legal system that is both compliant and repressive, a party system in which one party, whether in opposition or in the majority, is bent upon reconstituting the existing system so as to permanently favor a ruling class of the wealthy, the well-connected and the corporate, while leaving the poorer citizens with a sense of helplessness and political despair, and, at the same time, keeping the middle classes dangling between fear of unemployment and expectations of fantastic rewards once the new economy recovers. That scheme is abetted by a sycophantic

and increasingly concentrated media; by the integration of universities with their corporate benefactors; by a propaganda machine institutionalized in well-funded think
tanks and conservative foundations; by the increasingly closer cooperation between
local police and national law enforcement agencies aimed at identifying terrorists,
suspicious aliens and domestic dissidents.

(Wolin 2003)

Wolin does a good job in connecting the war on terror to the development of this
"inverted" form of totalitarianism in the United States. The bombings on 9/11 have
become, in an anthropological sense, sacralized—i.e., the day is holy and, by extension,
the war on terror is a sacred undertaking (2008: 5). But if the war on terror is now sacred
then terror itself must also be sacred, providing a whole new meaning to "holy terror."
The idea of sacred terror does not make much sense on the surface but anthropologists
and sociologists know that the sacred is actually double sided: where there is good there
is evil. Sociologists have named this demarcation the line between the "sacred pure" and
the "sacred impure" (Durkheim 1995 [1912]) and will sometimes use curious formula-
tions to denote the "identity" or essential connection of good and evil, with phrases such
as gods being "positive devils" and devils being "negative gods." Gods and devils: two
sides of the same coin. You cannot have one without the other. Of course, we could have
neither (where we realize that "it's just us," and that we are alone in the world without
need for imaginary supplements), but this condition is rarely found in history (see
Greenblatt 2011: 69–72; Weber 1930: 61). Societies, it would seem, actually do need
imaginaries and a moral surplus like terrorism is a perfect imaginary supplement to the
new world of inverted totalitarianism (Hedges 2010).

Lacking a major existential threat such as the Soviet Union during the Cold War the
current U.S. imperial system would have to rest its justifications on its own bare material calculations such as war for oil, etc., but these justifications do not flush with
America's professed democratic idealism. Wolin reveals how the war on terror functions to legitimate US **imperialism** and unlimited military expansion.

By declaring a war on terrorism, America had, in the pastoral language of its
president, found "its mission and its moment." In his message urging the expansion of the government's powers under the intrusive Patriot Act, the president
turned from his New Testament friendly god to assume the role of the Old
Testament god of vengeance and wrath, vowing, "We will never forget the serv-
ants of evil who plotted the attacks and we will never forget those who rejoiced at
our grief."

"The struggle against global terrorism," according to the administration's National
Security Strategy (NSS), "is different from any other war in our history. It will
be fought on many fronts against a particularly elusive enemy over an extended
period of time.'" The characteristics of the hastily constructed new world were like

terrorism, vague and indeterminate. "The war against terrorists of global reach," according to NSS, "is a global enterprise of uncertain duration."

(2008: 72)

But what if we don't feel as if we live in a totalitarian regime? Do not most of us subjectively feel free? If America had "gone fascist" should we not be able to discern that fairly easily and without any assistance?

The Protestant Reformation certainly expressed many progressive trends but the "father" of the Reformation, Martin Luther, was not quite the "radical" or progressive he is often portrayed. Luther's new slant on political theology divided the person into two distinct aspects: the internal and the external or, to put it another way, the objective and the subjective. Luther's theology made it possible for a person to live the life of a slave in a forced-labor camp (McCarthy 2006: 122) all the while believing they are free. In other words, our bodies can be working in a hell while our heads are dreaming of a heavenly existence. Freedom, therefore, takes on a "schizophrenic" quality. With Luther:

> freedom was assigned to the "inner sphere of the person, to the 'inner' man, and at the same time the 'outer' person was subjected to the system of worldly powers; this system of earthly authorities was transcended through private autonomy and reason; person and work were separated ... with the resultant 'double morality'; actual unfreedom and inequality were justified as a consequence of 'inner' freedom and equality."

(Marcuse 1972: 56)

Not only does it become difficult to know if we are free (either positively or negatively), but we are also disconnected at the level of belief and action. It is possible, then, that Americans can get up every day and go to work believing all the while that they are free, they live in a democracy, they are doing just what they want to do, are "getting ahead" and so on while, in fact, they are only doing what they would be forced to do otherwise, and that is get up every day and participate in voluntary human sacrifice for their corporate masters. Moral notions like terror (along with a-thousand-and-one other moral representations) work to lubricate the irresolvable conflict between what we think we are doing and what we are actually doing. There is a lot of money to be made off the backs of a mystified population at war with evil.

The Business of Terror

> Well, you hear a lot of talk these days about homeland security. Sounds to me like someone's going to make some serious money out of it ... in the usual way.
>
> (Ry Cooder, from "Spayed Kooley," *I, Flathead* (2008), Nonesuch Records)

How many dollars has America spent on the war against terror? It is entirely possible that we will never really know. Everything is secret and what information is presented to the public is grossly incomplete and even intentionally misleading, with security funds hidden in the budgets of agencies and bureaucracies lacking a security orientation. The Eisenhower Study Group's Cost of War project at Brown University puts forward a "moderate" estimate of partial outlays of roughly $4,000,000,000,000 for the first ten years (Watson Institute 2011). Four trillion dollars is a lot of money, but even this number fails to encompass the entire cost structure—the list of items left out of the Cost of War estimates is quite long. The cost, like most aspects of this "war," might as well be thought of as "unlimited." Americans fell for this war because it seemed imperative to survival.

> Having been given a steady diet of vague but terrifying information from national security officials about the possibility of dirty bombs, chemical weapons, biotoxins, exploding airliners, and suicide bombers, a nation of men and women … have shelled out hundreds of billions [of] dollars to turn the machine of government over to defeating terrorism without ever really questioning what they were getting for their money. And even if they did want an answer to that question, they would not be given one, both because those same officials have decided it would gravely harm national security to share such classified information—and because the officials themselves don't actually know.
>
> (Priest and Arkin 2011: xviii–xix)

When we consider domestic homeland security costs, we might as well tack on an additional one trillion dollars for the ten years following 9/11 (Mueller and Stewart 2011). What is all this money going to and to whom?

The Department of Homeland Security projected budget for fiscal year 2013 is 59 billion dollars (DHS 2011). How DHS money is spent and how much is spent is not actually known. Total 2010 assets are listed at over 90 billion dollars and total liabilities are listed at nearly 83.6 billion dollars, but we are forced to take their word for it when it comes to outlays because DHS financial reports are not subjected to auditing even though they are supposed to be; the 2010 "Annual Financial Report" indicates that the whole thing, in fact, is "unaudited" and the word "unaudited" appears 330 times in the 202-page document (DHS 2010). Dollars and cents aside, this much is not in dispute: terror is good business for American firms. When President Bush raised allocations for homeland security in 2002 (an initial $38 billion), businesses and government agencies (which spend money on wages, goods, and services) lined up "to grab their shares of the federal spending. Just as the Cold War spurred enormous expenditures on bomb shelters, an interstate highway system and education programs, homeland security has become a growth industry" (Miller and Pianin 2002: 4A). And just as business relies on terror, terrorist groups do not operate on ideology alone.

It takes money to wage war against empires and terrorist groups are dedicated not only to wiping out their enemies but raising funds for materials, personnel, training, and communications. Each group is unique, so it would be impossible, here, with limited space, to delve into any detail. However, as an aside, it is interesting that in its heyday and before bin Laden was killed, some folks with a business eye reframed Al Qaeda as "nimble, highly flexible start-ups trying to undermine" nations states conceived as larger businesses and suggested that terrorist operations offered "lessons" that legitimate firms could learn from (Weber 2004).

DISCUSSION QUESTIONS

1. Has the United States been transformed into an authoritarian regime?
2. How does "inverted totalitarianism" differ from classical totalitarianism?
3. Is the war on terror worth the trillions of dollars and thousands of lives it has cost?
4. How does the "spiritual aroma" of Protestantism (i.e., the splitting of the person into the subjective and the objective as well as the onerous duty to obey) help to enable a disconnection between how Americans act and how they think of their freedoms?

IV: The Terror of Empire and the Empire of Terror

~~~~~~

Beginning around 1900 the United States began its specifically imperialist–hegemonic career. The energy and resources necessary to sustain this expansion were acquired by a combination of external extractions and domestic repression. America was set on a perpetual collision course with other states and sub-state actors. The United States passed through at least three great economic phases since the turn of the 20th century: the pre-Fordist era of robber barons and tycoons; the Fordist era of mass manufacturing and strong labor unions from the end of World War I to the early 1970s, and the post-Fordist era of de-industrialization and the reign of speculation. It is this latest phase that will interest us because the Age of Terror coincides exactly with the birth of the post-Fordist regime of capital accumulation and the necessity to support the dollar with the fear of annihilation. This is important: in the industrial phase there was a greater correspondence between money and the amount of value within a system expressed in commodities manufactured by workers. Value coincides with the amount of labor time it takes to make an object. What happens, though, when the money supply grossly exceeds the amount of actual value in a system and, especially, when money begins to "float" freely unimpeded by something like a gold tether? In 2007 the amount of value in the global derivatives market was estimated to be one *quadrillion* dollars. "This is ten times the total worth, adjusted for inflation, of all the products made by the world's manufacturing industries over the last century" (Stewart 2012). Obviously, there is not enough physical money in existence to represent that quantity of value. When we move into the realm of quadrillions of dollars we are moving in a kind of substanceless ether where the value that money reflects is purely fictional. This is a world where prices have become divorced from values and float around on their own (for more see McNally 2011). How, then, does a state or an empire keep an economy going when it is based on supporting a massive, limitless fiction built far and above the bedrock of actual value? Enter the Department of Defense. Marx's concepts of use-value and exchange-value will, in the future, need to be supplemented with concepts of uselessness-value and fear-value.

The Imperial State and Terror: The Weird Polarity

There is often an odd connection between polar extremes such as the very big and the very little, and imperialism carries this logic of asymmetrical polarity to an extreme: the wealthiest nation bulldozing the poorest into rubble; Private McSkills operating advanced weapons systems; a state with the power to destroy all life on earth with nuclear weapons resorting to torture (Hardt and Negri 2004: 18–19); and the bond that connects the fundamentalist true believer in Jesus Christ as personal lord and savior and the impersonal corporation with a fundamentalist's zeal for quarterly profits. This last polarity deserves a few words:

> The odd couple of Superpower is an alliance that finds reactionary, backward-looking archaic forces (economic, religious, and political) allied with forward-looking forces of radical change (corporate leaders, technological innovators, scientists (whose efforts contribute to steadily distancing contemporary society from its past. It is as though the archaist believes that by going forward, by allying with dynamic powers, he enables an ever-receding past somehow to bring the revelation closer.
> (Wolin 2008: 117)

It is specifically the spirit of anomie that holds this bizarre fusion of profane corporate imperialism and religious primitivism together. Corporate imperialism might as well be named "Chaos Incorporated," and it is chaos, the imagined reign of Satan, that drives the fundamentalist Christian toward the post-apocalyptic utopia. "Millennial hopes mix with other elements in the totalitarian dynamic to feed an impulse toward limitlessness" (ibid.). It is this "limitlessness" that conjoins, here, the holy and the unholy, the sacred and the profane, the empire of capital with the empire of Christ. Last but not least, the imperial state and the terrorist also form a symbiotic, asymmetrical polarity—where you find one you will find the other. The terrorist is the empire in its "negative" and individuated form and empire is terrorism in its "positive" and aggregated form. Earlier we could not make up our mind about the notion of "state terror" but we may be in a better position at this point to reveal more.

State Terror: Another View

The United States is essentially a liberal bourgeois nation, but from the New Deal to about the early 1970s the United States was also characterized by a balance of countervailing powers including a genuine capital–labor accord that was partially responsible for the realization of the "American Dream" for millions of people and the growth of a large and well-off middle class. From the end of the seventies, however, labor unions were crushed, markets were deregulated, war after war transferred ever greater quantities of power to the executive branch of the federal government as well as to the Department of Defense, and importantly, the growing power and influence of the speculation–defense nexus amounts to nothing less than the seizure of the state for the benefits of a few (Wolin 2003).

Under these conditions can we say that it is correct to classify state violence carried out in the name of all but in reality for the benefit of a particular and statistically insignificant segment of the population as terrorist? I think so. The violence perpetrated by the U.S. government, including the violence that it sponsors around the globe, is of a terrorist nature fluffed up with fancy rhetoric and bankrolled on the fading glory of America, the land of the free. The invasion of Iraq is a perfect example.

When the United States preemptively invaded Iraq it reduced that nation to a parking lot on trumped-up charges and gross fabrications swirling around weapons of mass destruction and links to terrorists. In reality, the utter annihilation of Iraq was a premeditated payback for decades of disobedience and, partially, the threat that Iraq could have posed for dollar stability (see Worrell 2011).

Globalization and the Military–Industrial–Speculative Complex

Holy wars are really ideological wars and, in the final analysis, ideological wars come down to objective, non-ideological resources (Park cited in Turner 1967: 164). The United States was once an industrial powerhouse but, now, its greatest export, after garbage and scrap (Humes 2012), is the dollar, used as the global reserve currency and primary medium of international exchange. "Fully 85% of foreign-exchange transactions world-wide are trades of other currencies for dollars .... The greenback, in other words, is not just America's currency. It's the world's" (Eichengreen 2011). A number of factors contribute to the dollar's stability as the global currency: it is convenient, safe, and lacks many alternatives (ibid.). The perceived "moral leadership" projected by the United States since the end of World War II (we did defeat the Nazis, fascism, and communism after all), as well as the fear of mutual financial destruction, also drives the reign of the dollar.

> Since 1968 the key pressure point has been the readiness of US diplomats to play the role of world wreckers if foreign central banks stop relending their dollar inflows to the US Treasury. This is the monetary equivalent of President Nixon's "mad bomber" threat, metastasized into the financial sphere: If the United States does not get its way, it will act irascibly and quite likely irrationally, and the world will suffer.
> (Hudson 2003: 387)

How could the failure of the U.S. economy or the dollar signal widespread economic disaster?

Hudson thinks of the United States as a "monetary imperialism" that has gained the upper hand in the post-war era by becoming a debtor nation. Ditching the gold standard in 1971 and running up the national debt, issuing trillions of dollars worth of Treasury bills,

> has enabled the United States to draw on the resources of the rest of the world without reciprocation, governing financially through its debtor position, not through its

creditor status. As dollar debts have replaced gold as the backing for central bank reserves, and hence for the world's credit supply, the entire system would be threatened if questions into its intrinsic unfairness were reopened.

(ibid.: 377)

Aligning so-called Third-World central bank policies with U.S. interests and enriching local elites ("puppet regimes") the United States maintains its dollar hegemony. But other forces keep the dollar on top. America's military prowess has little to do with making the world safe for democracy; rather, the "investments" in defense are designed to uphold America's monetary supremacy. If U.S. financial policy is "economically suicidal" to other nations (ibid.: 388), then how can we force these nations to commit to their own self-destruction? The long-term, parasitic extraction of wealth is preferable to being destroyed like Iraq. Signaling an intent to injure dollar hegemony will get a nation reclassified as a member of the Axis of Evil and be returned to the Stone Age post-haste.

The war on terror that crystallized in the aftermath of 9/11 was to a great extent articulated as a legitimating framework for a neoconservative and neoliberal project of capitalist globalization and the unabated and perhaps accelerated transfer of wealth from the periphery to the imperial core. Fear of Islam and the fanatical Muslim were cultivated for the benefit of Western power elites.

> Since the events of 9/11 the West in general and the USA in particular have used the specter of Islam as our excuse and justification for our foreign (and domestic) policies. That cataclysmic event vaulted a neo-conservative world view front and center, which lead to a willingness to use military power unilaterally and without regard to international norms in order to rectify and restore American and European interests as the US Government has defined them. Our official understanding of anti-western terrorism is that it is a direct result of Islam's rejection of western liberalism and a rejection of the freedom and conspicuous consumption of non-Islamic nations. By framing the response as a "war on terrorism" the US Government obscures the anti-communal nature of its position .... I mean that **neo-liberalism** rejects the rights of those who embody difference even as it purports to defend a system of democracy rooted in difference.
>
> (Fasenfest 2011: 381; bold added; see glossary)

To a very great extent the war on terror is an ideology that covers over or masks a simple money grab and control. The United States keeps pumping money into the global economy and holds a gun to the heads of loaner nations, e.g., China, forcing them to keep buying the debt "or else." In response to the Federal Reserve's "quantitative easing" (QE) or pumping hundreds of billions of dollars into the economy, China's Premiere "left no doubt ... that China is irked by Washington's response to the credit crunch, suspecting that the US is engaging in a stealth default on its debt by driving down the dollar. 'We have lent a massive amount of capital to the United States, and of course we are concerned about the security of our assets'" (Evans-Pritchard 2009).

After round two (QE2) was announced on November 3, 2010, Yeonpyeong Island was shelled by North Korean (proxy) artillery on November 23, and before the end of the year a photo of China's new J-20 stealth fighter (in a jaunty pose displaying a large red star) was leaked to the press. Was China signaling to the United States that more "quantitative easing" would not be tolerated? There is no proof and they could be merely coincidental, yet what is not in doubt is the fact that war in the postmodern world is conducted not only against enemies but also against "allies" and trading partners. In short, the classic political theology distinction between friend and foe may be melting down into an ambiguous amalgam. The specter of terror is a reflection of this bizarre fusion. The United States is going its own way and everybody on earth is on the wrong side. The only way to avoid being ground under is to loan the United States money, conduct transactions using dollars, denominate reserves in dollars, provide land for military bases, buy American weapon systems or other exports including our trash, and provide U.S. citizens with low-priced goods. Cooperation leads to stagnation and financial crises but disobedience leads to destruction.

DISCUSSION QUESTIONS

1. What role does the military play in supporting Wall Street?
2. How does the "spirit" of anomie bind together profane corporate drives and religious fanaticism?
3. Is the primary role of the military to "defend democracy" or to defend the interests of a minority class of elites?
4. How does the United States extract wealth from other nations via debt?

V: Conclusion

Terrorism is very simple from one angle: terrorists are just angry fanatics killing people and destroying things for revenge. However, beneath this uncomplicated veneer lies a bewildering complexity that impinges on virtually every aspect of contemporary life. At the most aggregate level we must see that America is at war with the world, the whole world, even its allies. This war can assume the form of military conflict where we destroy whole nations (Iraq) or wage a war on a supposedly "allied" nation that we sell weapons to (Pakistan)—oddly, the military mission in Afghanistan also involves a war on a segment of the Pakistani regime (see Worrell 2011). The war against the world is also an economic struggle. The United States will be incapable of sustaining its growth unless it receives ever-greater streams of tribute from creditors as well as a steady stream of energy and low-priced consumables. The Organization of Petroleum Exporting Countries (OPEC) made the mistake of disobedience in the seventies and, for that, the entire Middle East had a boot on its throat for a whole generation. When the war in Iraq failed to pan out the way the United States had anticipated, and the Arab Spring deposed key dictators aligned with U.S. interests, the focus shifted ("tilted") toward Asia and Australia. Why? The United States is attempting to encircle China and put a noose around its neck. From the political–economic view that is what the war on terror comes down to (whether the phrase is used or dropped for expediency). When we peer into the fine-grain details of terror and terrorists, however, the picture is more complicated because the details involve not just the nuts and bolts of organization but social psychology on both sides of the equation: us and them.

The social psychological theory of terrorism I posited involves three main currents: anomie, authoritarianism, and destructiveness. These three concepts are central ideas that come from the worlds of interpretive and critical sociology. When we locate these currents operating at the level of the individual mind we find a lack of coherence, but when we move up the scale of social organization and human assemblage we find that they crystallize into, for our purposes, two distinct formations. On the one side (let us call it the imperial side), anomie, authoritarianism, and destructiveness synthesize into what we have called sociological heterarchy. On the other side (let us call it the terrorist side), anomie, authoritarianism, and destructiveness come together to form what we have called piacularism. Heterarchy and piacularism are twin, distinct, yet interdigitated manifestations of the same logic: our "progress" is measured by their "regress"; our egoism is mirrored by their altruism; fears and hatred comingle in distorted images; and our stagnant wages are compensated symbolically with terror and subsidized economically by deficit spending and cheap labor—and their stagnation is measured in fanatical self-destruction.

The limitless spirit of a behemoth and its violent expansion produces many "by-products" and symptoms, one of which is its tiny but "spectacular" double, its homunculus, the terrorist. Just as the behemoth is everywhere (sea, air, land, outer space, and cyberspace) the terrorist must also be imagined to be "everywhere." Wherever "we" go it will follow. The image of the "terrorist" as homunculus is apt because, like the homunculus in Goethe's *Faust*, the terrorist is a synthetic, miniature product that empire has grown dependent upon for its survival and, that, in its enthusiastic self-destruction unites that which otherwise remains asunder (Goethe 1976: 172–214).

> Not one but grudges sovereign rule
> To others, most to him who seized it by his strength
> And strongly reigns. For he who has not learnt to rule
> His inner self, is only too intent to rule
> His neighbor's will to suit his own imperious mind.

(ibid.: 177)

Terror is designed to attack the "spiritual" domain (collective and personal consciousness and unconsciousness) and, like propaganda, is successful when it blends together ideas like peace and war. As such, "the last stronghold of free souls" is attacked and the prospects for peace are obliterated. Peace is war and war is peace (Park cited in Turner 1967: 149). From this point of view we must conclude that terrorism, unfortunately, "works" as a spiritual reality that undermines the basic tenets of modern liberal society. Another way of thinking about terror and the war on terror is to place it alongside other ideological movements that serve authoritarian state functions. Antisemitism in Nazi Germany functioned as a substitute for internal class conflict (Neumann 1944). In the United States antisemitism and other less mystical forms of racism were rampant and also functioned to displace class conflict to another dimension during the thirties and forties when capitalism was on the ropes (Worrell 2008). The ideologies of "the American Dream" and *especially* anticommunism both worked to stabilize post-war American society and dissipate anticapitalist energies. Today, when capitalism and its pathologies are being scrutinized like no other time since the thirties, it is the war on terror that is operating to keep the collective gaze fixed on the *bête noir* of the radical Islamofascist rather than on the roots of our problems. Capitalism and war go together like beer and pizza.

Some "fanatics" are pushed to the fringes of their societies where they aspire to shift the order of power through violent means, and in some societies "fanatics" actually assume the levers of power and do transform the global relations of power... There is no general formula for terror and terrorism but in the case of the American war on terror we clearly see the speculative mirroring and conflict between two antagonistic and fanatical projects.

The entire world is suffering through a tremendous and complicated emergency that assumes economic, political, religious, and cultural aspects. If the situation is to improve or if the problem is to be actually solved then our common ideas and intellectual frameworks will have to be junked for new, critical terms. Terror and war on terror are two such terms that, far from assisting us to comprehend the current state of affairs, actually stun or agitate the populace, enabling the prolongation of the status quo. Phrases like "war on terror" are "false terms, mystifying our perception of the situation instead of allowing us to think it" (Zizek 2012).

References

Adams, James. 1986. *The Financing of Terror*. New York: Simon.

Adorno, T. W., E. Frenkel-Brunswik, D. J. Levinson, and R. N. Sanford. 1950. *The Authoritarian Personality*. New York: Harper.

Aho, James. 1994. *This Thing of Darkness*. Seattle: University of Washington Press.

Ali, Farhana and Jerrold Post. 2008. "The History and Evolution of Martyrdom in the Service of Defensive Jihad." *Social Research 75(2)*: 615–54.

Altemeyer, Bob. 1996. *The Authoritarian Specter*. Cambridge: Harvard University Press.

———. 2006. *The Authoritarians*. Retrieved December 28, 2011 (http://home.cc.umanitoba.ca/~altemey).

American Bar Association. 2006. "Blue Ribbon Task Force Finds President Bush's Signing Statements Undermine Separation of Powers." Retrieved April 16, 2012 (http://www.abanow.org/2006/07/blue-ribbon-task-force-finds-president-bushs-signing-statements-undermine-separation-of-powers).

Anti-Defamation League. 2005. "A Decade after Oklahoma City Bombing, Domestic Terrorism Threat Still Looms." Retrieved December 29, 2011 (www.adl.org/learn/extremism_in_the_news/Anti_Government/okc_10years_40805.htm).

Baehr, Peter. 2009. "The Novelty of Jihadist Terror." *Society 46*: 210–13.

Bailey, Ronald. 2006. "Don't be Terrorized." Retired April 6, 2012 (http://reason.com/archives/2006/08/11/dont-be-terrorized).

Bell, Daniel. 1963. "The Dispossessed." Pp. 1–45 in *The Radical Right*, ed. Daniel Bell. Garden City: Anchor.

Brzezinski, Zbigniew. 2007. "Terrorized by 'War on Terror.'" *Washington Post*, March 25. Retrieved May 9, 2012 (http://www.washingtonpost.com/wp-dyn/content/article/2007/03/23/AR2007032301613.html).

Butler, Smedley D. 2003. *War is a Racket*. Port Townsend: Feral House.

Centers for Disease Control and Prevention (CDC) 2009. "Leading Causes of Death." Retrieved April 6, 2012 (http://www.cdc.gov/nchs/fastats/lcod.htm).

Centers for Disease Control and Prevention (CDC) 2011. "Homicides—United States, 1999–2007." Retrieved April 6, 2012 (http://www.cdc.gov/mmwr/preview/mmwrhtml/su6001a14.htm).

Chomsky, Noam. 1989. *Necessary Illusions*. Boston: South End Press.

Churchill, Ward. 2003. *On the Justice of Roosting Chickens*. Oakland: AK Press.

Cooder, Ry. 2008. "Spayed Kooley. In *I, Flathead*. New York: Nonesuch Records.

Cottam, Martha L., Beth Dietz-Uhler, Elena Mastors, and Thomas Preston. 2010. *Introduction to Political Psychology*, 2nd edition. New York: Psychology Press.

Crenshaw, Martha. 1995. "Thoughts on Relating Terrorism to Historical Contexts." Pp. 3–24 in *Terrorism in Context*, ed. Martha Crenshaw. University Park: Pennsylvania State University Press.

———. 2011. *Explaining Terrorism*. London and New York: Routledge.

Dean, John W. 2006. *Conservatives without Conscience*. New York: Viking.

Department of Homeland Security. 2010. "Department of Homeland Security Fiscal Year 2010 Annual Financial Report." Retrieved May 9, 2012 (http://www.dhs.gov/xlibrary/assets/cfo-afrfy2010-vol2.pdf).

———. 2011. "Budget-in-Brief: Fiscal Year 2013." Retrieved May 9, 2012 (http://www.dhs.gov/xlibrary/assets/mgmt/dhs-budget-in-brief-fy2013.pdf).

Diamond, Sara. 1995. *Roads to Dominion*. New York: Guilford Press.

Dingley, James. 2010. *Terrorism and the Politics of Social Change*. Farnham: Ashgate.

Durkheim, Emile. 1915. *Germany Above All*. Paris: Librairie Armand Colin.

———. 1951 [1897]. *Suicide*. New York: Free Press.

———. 1974. *Sociology and Philosophy*, trans. D. F. Pocock. New York: Free Press.

———. 1984 [1893]. *The Division of Labor in Society*. New York: Free Press.

———. 1995 [1912]. *The Elementary Forms of Religious Life*, trans. Karen E. Fields. New York: Free Press.

Eichengreen, Barry. 2011. "Why the Dollar's Reign is Near an End." *Wall Street Journal*, March 1. Retrieved May 10, 2012 (http://online.wsj.com/article/SB10001424052748703313304576132170181013248.html).

Evans-Pritchard, Ambrose. 2009. "China Fears Bond Crisis as it Slams Quantitative Easing." *Telegraph*, May 6. Retrieved May 10, 2012 (http://www.telegraph.co.uk/finance/newsbysector/banksandfinance/5286832/China-fears-bond-crisis-as-it-slams-quantitative-easing.html).

Fasenfest, David. 2011. "Terrorism, Neo-Liberalism and Political Rhetoric." *Critical Sociology* 37(4): 379–82.

Fromm, Erich. 1941. *Escape from Freedom*. New York: Henry Holt.

———. 1959. *Sigmund Freud's Mission*. New York: Grove Press.

——— and Michael Maccoby. 1996 [1970]. *Social Character in a Mexican Village*. New Brunswick: Transaction Publishers.

Fussell, Paul. 1996. *Doing Battle*. Boston: Little, Brown and Co.

Gerth, Hans and C. Wright Mills. 1953. *Character and Social Structure*. New York: Harcourt, Brace & World.

Gibbs, Jack P. 1989. "Conceptualization of Terrorism." *American Sociological Review* 54(3): 329–40.

Go, Julian. 2011. *Patterns of Empire*. Cambridge: Cambridge University Press.

Godlove, Terry F. 2005. *Teaching Durkheim*. New York: Oxford University Press.

Goethe, Johann Wolfgang von. 1976. *Faust*, trans. Walter Arndt. New York: W. W. Norton.

Goodstein, Laurie. 2001. "After the Attacks: Finding Fault." *New York Times*, September 15. Retrieved May 3, 2012 (http://www.nytimes.com/2001/09/15/us/after-attacks-finding-fault-falwell-s-finger-pointing-inappropriate-bush-says.html).

Goodwin, Jeff. 2006. "A Theory of Categorical Terrorism." *Social Forces 84(4)*: 2027–46.

Greenblatt, Stephen. 2011. *The Swerve*. New York: W. W. Norton.

Grimmett, Richard F. 2010. "Instances of Use of United States Armed Forces Abroad, 1798–2009." *Congressional Research Service*. Retrieved May 3, 2012 (http://www.fas.org/sgp/crs/natsec/RL32170.pdf).

Hardt, Michael and Antonio Negri. 2004. *Multitude*. New York: Penguin.

Hedges, Chris. 2006. *American Fascists*. New York: Free Press.

———. 2010. "Democracy in America is a Useful Fiction." Retrieved April 14, 2012 (http://www.truthdig.com/report/item/democracy_in_america_is_a_useful_fiction_20100124).

Hegel, G. W. F. 1977. *The Phenomenology of Spirit*, trans. A. V. Miller. Oxford: Oxford University Press.

Hersh, Seymour M. 2008. "Preparing the Battlefield." *New Yorker*, July 7/14: 61–67.

Hitchens, Christopher. 2007. "Defending Islamofascism." *Slate*. Retrieved April 16, 2012 (http://www.slate.com/articles/news_and_politics/fighting_words/2007/10/defending_islamofascism.html).

Hoffman, Bruce. 1984. *Right-Wing Terrorism in Europe*. Santa Monica: Rand.

Hubert, Henri and Marcel Mauss. 1964 [1898]. *Sacrifice*. Chicago: University of Chicago Press.

Hudson, Michael. 2003. *Super Imperialism*, 2nd edition. London: Pluto.

Humes, Edward. 2012. *Garbology*. New York: Penguin.

Johnson, Chalmers. 2004. *Blowback*. New York: Henry Holt.

Joyner, James. 2012. "Why the Obama Administration's Drone War May Soon Reach a Tipping Point." *New Republic*. Retrieved May 8, 2012 (http://www.tnr.com/article/world/103059/unmanned-aerial-vehicles-foreign-policy-drone-war-yemen).

Juergensmeyer, Mark. 2008. "Martyrdom and Sacrifice in a Time of Terror." *Social Research 75(2)*: 417–34.

Kellner, Douglas. 2003. *From 9/11 to Terror War*. Lanham: Rowman & Littlefield.

Krier, Dan. 2005. *Speculative Management*. Albany: State University of New York Press.

———. 2008. "Critical Institutionalism and Financial Globalization." *New York Journal of Sociology 1(1)*. Retrieved June 14, 2012 (www.newyorksociology.org).

Laqueur, Walter. 1999. *The New Terrorism*. New York: Oxford University Press.

Lukes, Steven. 1973. *Emile Durkheim*. Stanford: Stanford University Press.

MacAskill, Ewen. 2005. "The Suicide Bomber is the Smartest of Smart Bombs." *The Guardian*, July 13. Retrieved January 5, 2012 (http://www.guardian.co.uk/uk/2005/jul/14/israel.july7).

McCarthy, Cormac. 2006. *The Sunset Limited*. New York: Vintage.

McCauley, Clark and Sophia Moskalenko. 2011. *Friction: How Radicalization Happens to Them and Us*. New York: Oxford University Press.

McNally, David. 2011. *Monsters of the Market*. Leiden: Brill.

Mahanta, Siddhartha. 2011. "Protest Like an Egyptian?" *Mother Jones*. Retrieved May 9, 2012 (http://www.motherjones.com/mojo/2011/02/wisconsin-middle-east-midwest).

Marcuse, Herbert. 1972. *From Luther to Popper*. London: Verso.

Marx, Karl. 1963. *The 18th Brumaire of Louis Bonaparte*. New York: International Publishers.

Miller, Bill and Eric Pianin. 2002. "Battling Terrorism Good for Business." *Wilmington Morning Star*, (February 12): 4A.

Mills, C. Wright. 1956. *The Power Elite*. Oxford: Oxford University Press.

Mueller, John and Mark G. Stewart. 2011. *Terror, Security, and Money*. New York: Oxford University Press.

National Counterterrorism Center. 2012. *2011 Report on Terrorism*. Washington, D.C.: Office of the Director of National Intelligence, National Counterterrorism Center. Retrieved June 12, 2012 (http://www.nctc.gov/docs/2011_NCTC_Annual_Report_Final.pdf).

Nelson, Leonard. 1957 [1917]. *Critique of Practical Reason*. Frankfurt: Verlag.

Neumann, Franz. 1944. *Behemoth*. Chicago: Ivan R. Dee.

Orr, Jackie. 2004. "The Militarization of Inner Space." *Critical Sociology 30(2)*: 451–81.

Pedahzur, Ami, Arie Perliger, and Leonard Weinberg. 2003. "Altruism and Fatalism: The Characteristics of Palestinian Suicide Terrorists." *Deviant Behavior 24*: 405–23.

Post, Jerrold M. 2007. *The Mind of the Terrorist*. New York: Palgrave Macmillan.

———, Keven G. Ruby, and Eric D. Shaw. 2002. "The Radical Group in Context." *Studies in Conflict and Terrorism 25*: 101–26.

Priest, Dana and William M. Arkin. 2011. *Top Secret America*. New York: Little, Brown and Co.

Rubenstein, Richard E. 1987. *Alchemists of Revolution*. New York: Basic Books.

Sahlins, Marshall. 1972. *Stone Age Economics*. New Brunswick: Aldine/Transaction.

Scott-Clark, Cathy and Adrian Levy. 2010. "How to Defuse a Human Bomb." *Guardian*, October 15. Retrieved January 1, 2012 (www.guardian.co.uk/world/2010/oct/16/defuse-human-bomb-taliban?INTCMP=SRCH).

Slotkin, Richard. 1973. *Regeneration Through Violence*. New York: Harper.

START. 2007. Retrieved April 6, 2012 (http://www.start.umd.edu/start).

Stern, Kenneth S. 1996. *A Force Upon the Plain*. New York: Simon & Schuster.

Stewart, David. 1989. "Hermeneutics of Suspicion." *Literature and Theology 3(3)*: 296–307.

Stewart, Ian. 2012. "The Mathematical Equation that Caused the Banks to Crash." *The Guardian*, February 11. Retrieved May 10, 2012 (http://www.guardian.co.uk/science/2012/feb/12/black-scholes-equation-credit-crunch).

Stone, William F., G. Lederer, and R. Christie. 1993. *Strength and Weakness*. New York: Springer-Verlag.

Strenski, Ivan. 2006. *The New Durkheim*. New Brunswick: Rutgers University Press.

Tilly, Charles. 2004. "Terror, Terrorism, Terrorists." *Sociological Theory 21(1)*: 5–13.

Trotsky, Leon. 2007 [1920]. *Terrorism and Communism*. London: Verso.

Turk, Austin T. 2004. "The Sociology of Terrorism." *Annual Review of Sociology 30*: 271–86.

Turner, Ralph H. (ed.). 1967. *Robert E. Park: On Social Control and Collective Behavior*. Chicago: University of Chicago Press.

Waller, James. 2002. *Becoming Evil*. New York: Oxford University Press.

Wasmund, Klaus. 1986. "The Political Socialization of West German Terrorists." Pp. 191–228 in *Political Violence and Terror*, ed. Peter Merkl. Berkeley: University of California Press.

Watson Institute. 2011. "Costs of War." Retrieved May 7, 2012 (http://costsofwar.org).

Weber, Max. 1930. *The Protestant Ethic and the Spirit of Capitalism*, trans. Talcott Parsons. London: Routledge.

Weber, Tim. 1952. *Ancient Judaism*, trans. Hans Gerth and Don Martindale. New York: Free Press.

———. 2004. "Do Terrorists Have a Business Plan?" BBC News, 23 January (http://news.bbc.co.uk/2/hi/business/3422925.stm).

Weinberg, Leonard. 1991. "Turning to Terror: The Conditions under which Political Parties Turn to Terrorist Activities." *Comparative Politics 23(4)*: 423–38.

——— and William Lee Eubank. 1988. "Neo-Fascist and Far Left Terrorists in Italy: Some Biographical Observations." *British Journal of Political Science 18(4)*: 531–49.

Wieviorka, Michel. 1995. "Terrorism in the Context of Academic Research." Pp. 597–606 in *Terrorism in Context*, ed. Martha Crenshaw. University Park: Pennsylvania State University Press.

Wolin, Sheldon. 2003. "Inverted Totalitarianism." *Nation*, May 19. Retrieved January 5, 2012 (www.thenation.com/article/inverted-totalitarianism).

———. 2008. *Democracy Incorporated*. Princeton: Princeton University Press.

Worrell, Mark P. 1998. "Critical Theory, Authoritarianism, and Political Psychology." *Social Thought and Research 21(1/2)*: 1–33.

———. 1999. "The Veil of Piacular Subjectivity." *Electronic Journal of Sociology 4(3)*. Retrieved May 2, 2012 (http://www.sociology.org/content/vol004.003/buchanan.html).

———. 2008. *Dialectic of Solidarity: Labor, Antisemitism, and the Frankfurt School.* Chicago: Haymarket.

———. 2011. *Why Nations Go to War: A Sociology of Military Conflict.* London and New York: Routledge.

Zakaria, Fareed. 2012. "US Has Made War on Terror a War without End." CNN. Retrieved May 8, 2012 (http://globalpublicsquare.blogs.cnn.com/2012/05/06/national-security-state).

Zedalis, Debra D. 2004. "Female Suicide Bombers." Strategic Studies Institute. Retrieved December 31, 2010 (www.strategicstudiesinstitute.army.mil/pdffiles/pub408.pdf).

Zenko, Micah. 2012. "Americans are as Likely to be Killed by Their Own Furniture as by Terrorism." *The Atlantic,* June 6. Retrieved June 12, 2012 (http://www.theatlantic.com/international/archive/2012/06/americans-are-as-likely-to-be-killed-by-their-own-furniture-as-by-terrorism).

Zizek, Slavoj. 2012. "Occupy Wall Street: What is to be Done Next." *The Guardian.* Retrieved April 24, 2012 (http://www.guardian.co.uk/commentisfree/cifamerica/2012/apr/24/occupy-wall-street-what-is-to-be-done-next).

Glossary/Index

9/11 9, 16, 17, 36
labeling of victims of 8–9
self-recrimination after 25–26

A
academic perspectives on terrorism 6–8
Afghanistan 9, 30, 32, 45
Al Qaeda: meaning "the base," as in a foundation or military base, Al Qaeda is an Islamic fundamentalist organization operating in and around Pakistan. Al Qaeda has conducted many attacks including bombing the World Trade Center in 1993, embassy bombings in Tanzania and Kenya in 1998, and the destruction of the World Trade Center towers, part of the Pentagon, and the crashing of another plane all on September 11, 2001 14, 15, 18, 39
Ali, Farhana 23
Altemeyer, Bob 12, 32
altruism 20, 21, 23
altruistic suicide 23, 24
American Bar Association 16
"American Dream" 41, 46
American terrorist movements 12–14
anomic suicide 23
anomie: deregulation, anarchy, or improper regulation. Anomie is usually found intimately bound together with egoism or excessive individuation. American sociology tends to render anomie as "normlessness," but this is misleading. Anomie points to a condition where once-prevailing norms lose their meaningful and energetic power of coercion and the responsibility of regulation is foisted back on the individual who is typically ill-equipped (sociologically incapable) of self-regulation (see Dingley 2010: 165 for a good presentation of anomie connected to suicide). Interestingly, it is the *futility* of self-regulation (that fusion known as "the disease of the infinite") that drives the transit from the dimension of "infinity" to its opposite dimension of finitude (where the self is transformed into an altruistic martyr) 3, 4, 21, 45

binding corporate drives and religious fanaticism 41

role in motives of suicide bombers 23

Anti-Defamation League 13

antisemitism 12, 13, 26, 46

Arab Spring: a dramatic wave of revolutions and lesser protests that swept across northern Africa and portions of the Middle East beginning in December 2010. The toppling of the dictatorial regime in Egypt was especially damaging to Israeli and American interests in the region 9, 45

Arkin, William 15, 38

asceticism: extreme self-renunciation, self-denial, and/or self-negation. Ascetic techniques such as self-mutilation, self-torture, and abstinence are used by people and groups to signify that they are "above suffering" (Durkheim 1995 [1912]: 400). Asceticism is related to piacular actions but the latter are used to signify not that one is "above suffering" but to signal that one is "in the grip of suffering" (ibid.). 25, 27

authoritarianism 4, 12, 14–15, 45

ideological movements serving state 46

in US 15–16, 18–19, 34–36

authority, terrorist opposition to established 13–14

B

Baehr, Peter 22

bin Laden, Osama: the son of Mohammed bin Awad bin Laden, a powerful businessman with strong ties to the Saudi royal family. Disowned by the bin Laden family, Osama was the leader of Al Qaeda, the supposed mastermind behind the September 11, 2001 terrorist attacks in America, and promoter of a theocratic form of Islamic government including the rule of sacred laws and holy war (jihad) against enemies of Islam. Osama bin Laden was shot and killed by US military and intelligence operatives during an early morning raid on his home in Abbottabad, Pakistan, on May 2, 2011 30

Black September 1

Brown, John: in 1859, the year he was executed, Brown famously led a paramilitary raid of antislavery volunteers into Harpers Ferry, Virginia in a bid to free and arm African-American slaves and launch a widespread liberation movement. Brown is one of the most controversial figures in all of American history, viewed by many as a hero and by others as a criminal terrorist. The national excitement generated by Brown and his execution was of tremendous importance in pushing America into civil war 7

Bush administration 10, 14, 15, 16

Bush, George W. 8, 9, 16, 19, 36, 38

business of terror 37–39

Butler, Smedley 31

C

capital: a form of money used to invest in machinery and laborers in order to produce goods and services for sale on a market. More broadly, anything bought for use in production, for exchange, including human time and energy, is converted into a form of capital. Human beings, therefore, working in a capitalist mode of production, are units of "variable capital"—variable, that is, in the amount to which they can be utilized in comparison with passive elements of production such as raw materials xi, xii, 1–2, 40

capitalism: involves value creation and the accumulation of surplus value through the production of commodities for exchange rather than needs-satisfaction. Radicals tend to lump all forms of wealth accumulation under the label of "capitalism" but we have to carefully distinguish between "capitalism" per se and "business," which can mean all kinds of moneymaking activities that now intersect with and then diverge from actual capitalism. Many speculative schemes and business adventures lead to the actual destruction of fixed capital assets and constitute what amounts to anticapitalism (see Krier 2005) xi, xii, 13, 21, 34, 43

Centers for Disease Control and Prevention (CDC) 33

character structure: a complex or syndrome of durable character traits or dispositions that form through socialization and adaptations to processes and structures prevailing in society. The "Protestant work ethic" is an example of an enduring characteristic at both the personal and impersonal levels 11

Chechen rebels 8

China 43–44, 45

civil liberties 16, 32, 34

climate change 2

Cold War 17, 38

concept of terrorism 5–10

consumption 10, 21

core and periphery 9–10, 32, 34, 43

cost of war on terror 38

Cost of War project 38

crime and war, terrorism in between concepts of 27–29

D

Dean, John 33–34

deaths 8, 22, 33

debt, American 42–44

decisionism 19

defining terrorism 5–6

democracy 16, 33–36, 37

Department of Homeland Security 30, 38

destructiveness 4, 14, 45

dollar 40, 42–44

Dominionism: a branch of extreme right-wing Christianity that takes its name from a passage in the biblical book of Genesis. Dominionism advocates a paradoxical mixture of economic and environmental anarchy, the imposition of a theocratic dictatorship, and the extreme repression of people who do not adhere to Dominionist ideals of probity 34

Dreyfus: Alfred Dreyfus was an officer in the French army who was wrongly accused and convicted of spying for the Germans in 1895. Dreyfus was locked up in Devil's Island prison from 1895 until 1899. Known as "the Dreyfus Affair," it is one of the most important controversies in the history of modern France and was one of the mainsprings for the idea of an independent Jewish state whereby Jews could escape centuries of European persecution 26

drone weapons 10, 30

Durkheim, E. 3, 13, 20, 21, 23, 24, 25, 26, 27, 36

E

economic phases 40

economy 40, 42–44, 45

elections 35

empire: an empire is "a sociopolitical formation wherein a central political authority (a king, a metropole, or imperial state) exercises unequal influence and power over the political (and in effect the sociopolitical) processes of a subordinate society, peoples, or space" (Go 2011: 7) 2, 41

expansion of 9, 17

modern hegemonic 2–3

US as an 2, 32, 40

eugenics, war as a form of 31

evil

concept of 19

"crusade" against 10

good and 3, 17, 19, 36

"other" 2, 14, 24, 26

exceptional moments 16

expiation: atonement for sinning or violation of some prohibition (taboo). The expiator is one who attempts to appease angry spirits, purify their self, others, or even the physical environment through ritual atonement 24

exports 42

F

fascism: a political system in which corporate interests are identical with government or state aims and whereby the corporate elite and their state use police and military coercion both internally and externally to further the interests of capital, business, and finance. Some critics of the US claim that while America still goes through the motions of being a democracy (holding sham elections and so on), it is now simply a fascist regime. "Fascism" is somewhat imprecise and is used more often than not as a pejorative rather than an analytic term 11, 34, 35

Fasenfest, David 43

fatalism: excessive regulation and despotic social control. In the modern world, fatalistic norms and control result in feelings of hopelessness, futility, and despair. 19
    role in motives of suicide bombers 22–23

fear of terror 33–34

features of terrorism 5–10

feminine terror 7–8

financial policy 40, 42–44

firearms 10

fitna 23

freedom xi, xii, 37

Fromm, Erich 11, 12, 14

G

globalization, project of capitalist 43

Goethe, Johann Wolfgang von 46

good and evil 3, 17, 19, 36

Goodwin, Jeff 6, 8

H

Hamas: born during the 1987 Intifada (rebellion against Israeli occupation of Palestinian territories), Hamas is a political, military, and religious party (defined by the United States as a terrorist organization) that currently controls the Gaza Strip 8

Hedges, Chris 2, 34, 36

Hegel, G.W.F. xii, 12, 21

hegemony: in a general sense hegemony is any kind of power that any social group (nation, status group, class, party) has over another group of whatever kind. This power can be economic, political, military, cultural, ideological, intellectual, etc. In a narrower sense, hegemony refers specifically to the economic power that a state has over other states or the globe. The United States is a global hegemon precisely in its reorganization and domination of the global economic order (see Go 2011: 7, 20). Only the United States (post-World War II) and Britain (19th century) have attained the status of both empires and hegemons in that they exert or exerted political and economic control over a complex of other nations (ibid.: 20) 17

heterarchy: in the sociological sense heterarchy is the paradoxical fusion of (a) full spectrum economic deregulation including financial chaos with (b) an atomized or over-individuated (egoistic) population mass and (c) domestic political futility, despotic police measures, and the massive buildup of a state security apparatus. Notions such as "libertarian fascism" point in the direction of the heterarchy concept. Constant war, mythical enemies at home and abroad, crime hysteria, mass incarceration, corporate propaganda, spectacle, celebrity worship, charismatic spectator politics, divide-and-conquer ideological polarization, and binge consumption via credit are a few of the mechanisms used by the Leviathan state to control its unwieldy population 5

radical 15, 22, 26, 43
Islamic Jihad 7, 9
"Islamofascism" 14, 15, 46

J
judiciary 16, 35
Juergensmeyer, Mark 24

K
Kellner, Douglas 10, 14–15, 17, 19
Ku Klux Klan: America's original terrorist organization consisting, at the height of its popularity in the early and mid-twenties, of up to perhaps 4,000,000 members. The "Klan" existed as multiple entities at various points in American history: after the American Civil War the KKK opposed reconstruction and promoted white supremacy; after World War I the Klan was not only opposed to racial integration but agitated against immigrants, Catholicism, communism, and basically any progressive feature of industrial capitalism; and finally, during the fifties and sixties the Klan agitated against the civil rights movement. Like other homegrown terrorist groups the Klan was all but destroyed by the FBI's counterterrorism efforts and today there are no more than a few thousand scattered adherents 13

L
labor unions 1, 9, 34, 41
Lebanese Civil War 7
limitlessness, spirit of 2, 41, 46
LTTE 8
Ludendorff, Erich von 9
Lukes, Steven 26
Luther, Martin 37

M
Marcuse, Herbert 37
Marines 31
martyrdom 24
military
   employment in 31
   failures 32, 35
   legitimizing unlimited expansion of 36–37
   prowess to uphold dollar hegemony 43
military–industrial–speculative complex 1, 42–44

Minutemen: an anticommunist guerrilla warfare group active throughout the sixties that Daniel Bell described as "small but insidious" and "willing to tear apart the fabric of American society in order to instate their goals" (Bell 1963: 45). Their goals were the eradication of communism (real and imagined) in the United States as well as the repression of Jews and blacks. Ironically, the federal government provided weapons to the National Rifle Association (NRA) for a marksmanship program and some of these weapons ended up with Minutemen terrorists who were NRA members (Stern 1996: 47–50) 13

N

neoconservativism: "Neocons" represent a sectarian right-wing political ideology centered on massive U.S. military power and global dominance all in the name of promoting freedom and democracy, i.e. democracy and freedom from the end of a bayonet. The plan to invade Iraq was one hatched by neoconservative think tanks in Washington, D.C. during the Clinton administration and was part of a larger plan for extending unrivaled U.S. military superiority over the nations of the world. Neoconservatism was a central ideological force guiding the Bush administration 16, 17, 43

neoliberalism: political–economic ideology that advocates privatization of public resources, unregulated free markets, and commercial anarchy. Despite the term neo*liberalism*, it is an ideology that goes down well with conservatives. Some view neoconservatism as neoliberalism with a gun 43

O

P

"Pax Americana" 17–18

Pedahzur, Ami 22–23

piacularism: a rite or ceremonial form of acting, thinking, and feeling that encompasses in-group purification and excitation in conjunction with the demonization and punishment of some out-group object that is deemed responsible for misfortunes that have befallen the group. These rites or ritual forms of conduct include self-negation either partially or totally (suicide) signifying, ultimately, the sacred and essential nature of the group. Piacular acts are driven by regressive anomic social conditions and evoke altruistic feelings and obligations for people to engage in sacrifice to bolster the fortunes of their society 5, 25–27, 45–46

polarities 4, 9–10, 40–41

political parties 28

political psychology 11–12, 15–16

political theology: Carl Schmitt believed that contemporary political concepts and categories are secular transfigurations of older religious ideas. For us, the decisive aspect is that politics is basically inseparable from notions of the sacred (both divine and diabolical) 16, 19, 37

Posse Comitatus: Latin for "power of the county," the Posse believes that all authority above the county level (e.g., Supreme Court and the rest of the federal government) is illegitimate 13

Post, Jerrold 1, 6, 23

postmodern terror 22

power elite: a small complex of key financiers and bankers, corporate movers and shakers (especially key figures in the defense industry), top military brass, select elected officials, some high-level career bureaucrats, a handful of powerful opinion-shapers in the media, as well as a handful of religious leaders and maybe even some celebrities. "Of the ... types ... that compose the power elite today, it is the military that has benefited the most in its enhanced power, although the corporate circles have also become more explicitly entrenched in the more public decision-making circles. It is the professional politician that has lost the most, so much that in examining the events and decisions, one is tempted to speak of a political vacuum in which the corporate rich and the high warlord, in their coinciding interests, rule" (Mills 1956: 276) 31, 43

premodern social organization 19–21, 22

premodern terror 20–21, 22

Priest, Dana 15, 38

"primitive modernism" 19

Project for a New American Century (PANC) 17

Protestant Reformation 37

R

S

T

Taliban: originally a movement of pious religious students (the name literally means "students") that came to power to govern Afghanistan until their overthrow in 2001, at which time they were converted into an insurgent group that operates in and around Pakistan attempting to regain lost ground against the United States 32

terrorists

American 12–14

in asymmetrical polarity with state 41

declaring war against 28–29

as homunculi 46

modern and post-modern 22

as "normal" 10

as radicals or reactionaries 11–12

raising funds 39

"will mania" of 3

Theater Center, Moscow 8

Tilly, Charles 7, 32

"Total War" 9

Trotsky 12

Turner, Ralph 9, 17, 42, 46

U

USA Patriot Act (2001) 36

V

victims 8–9, 25, 26

W

war

against allies and trading partners 44

as a form of eugenics 31

terrorism sitting between concepts of crime and 27–29

to uphold dollar hegemony 43

US dependency on 30–31, 36

and US difficulty in "winning" 18, 32, 35

war on terror 5, 30, 31–37

backfiring of 32

business of 37–39

either with US or against US in 16–17

erosion of democracy in 33–34, 36

instrument for domestic control xii, 16, 18–19, 32–34

legitimating imperialism and military expansion 36–37
masking an economic policy 43
no winning or losing in 18
under Obama administration 30
pretext for launch of "Pax Americana" 17–18
relationship of internal and external in 9–10
a sacred undertaking 10, 19, 36
serving authoritarian state functions 46
spending on 31, 38
violent authoritarianism on both sides in 14–15
"will mania" reflected in 3–4
Weber, Max 12, 20, 21, 25, 36
"will mania" 3–4
Wolin, Sheldon 16, 18, 35–36, 41
World War II 15, 17, 29
Worrell, Mark 12, 15, 25, 28, 30, 42, 45, 46

Z

Zakaria, Fareed 30
Zedalis, Debra 7, 8
"Zionist Occupation Government" ZOG) 13

THE SOCIAL ISSUES
COLLECTION™

University Readers™
Custom Publishing Evolved.

Routledge
Taylor & Francis Group

Finally, it's easy to
customize materials for your sociology course

Choose from a collection of 250 readings from Routledge and other
publishers to create a perfect anthology that fits your course and students.

1 Go to the website at
socialissuescollection.com

2 Choose from 250
readings in sociology

3 Create your complete
custom anthology

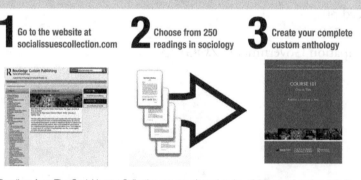

Readings from The Social Issues Collection are pre-cleared and available at reduced permission
rates, helping your students save money on course materials. Projects are ready in 2 weeks for
direct e-commerce student purchases.

For over 25 undergraduate sociology courses including:

Criminology

Cultural Sociology

Environmental Sociology

Gender

Globalization

Sociology of Work
and Economy

Marriage and Family

Race and Ethnicity

Social Inequalities

Sociology of Media
and Communication

Sociology of Place

Sociology of Religion

Contact us to learn more about our services

3970 Sorrento Valley Blvd. Ste 500, San Diego, CA 92121 I info@universityreaders.com I 800-200-3908 x 501

University Readers is an imprint of Cognella, Inc. ©1997-2012